FISHERMEN OF NOVA SCOTIA

FISHERMEN OF NOVA SCOTIA
L.B. Jenson

Petheric Press

It is an infringement of the author's rights and a violation of the copyright law to reproduce or utilize in any form or by any means electronic or mechanical, including photo copying, electrostatic copying, recording or by any information storage and retreival system or any other way, passages or drawings from this book without the **written permission of the publisher.**

First Edition
copyright 1980©
L. B. Jenson©
Second Printing 1984
Third Printing 1988

Published by
Petheric Press
division of Nimbus Publishing Limited
P.O. Box 9301, Station A
Halifax, N.S. B3K 5N5

Printed by
McCurdy Printing & Typesetting Limited,
Halifax, N.S. Canada

Canadian Cataloguing in Publication Data
Jenson, L.B., 1921 —
  Fishermen of Nova Scotia
ISBN 0-919380-33-6 pa.

1. Jenson L.B., 1921 —
Nova Scotia — Pictorial works.   2. Fishermen —
Nova Scotia — Pictorial works.   3. Fisheries —
5. Fisheries in art. I. Title.   4. Fishermen in art.

NC143.J46A4 1980   741.971   C80-094369-4

Drawings by L.B. Jenson marked with an asterick † are under Crown Copyright and now have been altered in some way for this book. Those marked * appear in previous Petheric Press Publications while those marked ‡ have been privately commissioned.

This drawing only indicates fish distribution in a general way. Most species may be found through the whole area. However, they have been caught commercially on a continuing basis by fishermen from various countries in the places indicated.

FISHERIES OF THE NORTH WEST ATLANTIC

Over 70% of the surface of the earth is covered by water. Fish is one of the most protein-rich foods known. It is consumed by only 1% of the world's population. Surely in the future the sea will provide food on the same scale as the land.

Based on "World Map of Fisheries" and "Atlas of the Oceans"

Fog is formed when warm, humid air blows in from the Gulf Stream over the cold Labrador Current which flows down the coasts of the Maritimes. Coming from seaward to the coast in a vessel, the bank of fog appears as a solid wall extending as far as can be seen.

L.B. JENSON

Contents

Page	General Subject
6	Setting the Scene
12	Early Discoveries in the North West Atlantic
24	From Colonial Times to the End of Sail
48	Whaling
52	Days of Transition
56	Side Trawling
59	Days of Rum and Fish Stores
65	Inshore Fishing Practices
70	Lobstering
74	Longlining
78	Seining
82	Weirs and Traps
86	Scallop Dragging
91	Stern Trawling
101	Seaweeds
102	Old Lunenburg
108	Lighthouses and Lifeboats
112	Russians, Oil Rigs & 200 Mile Fisheries Zone

THE SYMBOL OF THE WEALTH OF THE SEA

THE ATLANTIC COD
(Gadus morhua Linnaeus) — Cod, Codfish, morue commune, Cabillaud.

Place in History
The Codfish is one of the most important commercial resources found with the discovery of North America. A staple food since the Middle Ages, wars have been fought for cod-fishing grounds, countless lives and vessels have been sacrificed and great trading patterns established between nations. In 1976 Canadians caught nearly 200,000 metric tons of cod with a landed value of about $43,000,000!

General Characteristics
Cod usually live near the ocean floor & have been caught in water 6 feet in depth & as deep as 1,500 feet. They spawn in winter & each female lays 3 to 9 million eggs. About 2 to 9 eggs survive to adulthood. Eggs hatch in 2 or 3 weeks & the larvae feed on plankton. At 3 or 4 inches they descend to the bottom. They grow to adulthood eating mussels, crabs, squid & small fish.

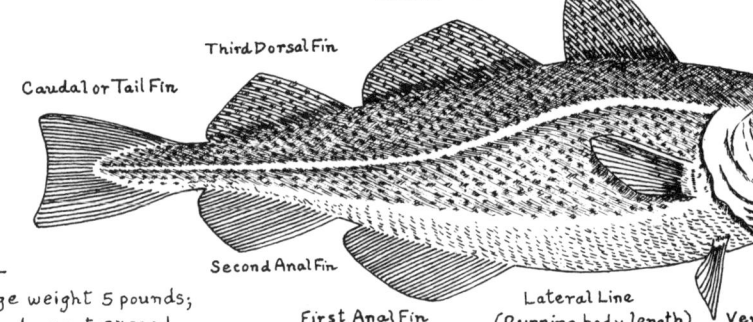

Body —
Body is elongate, stout, slightly compressed and tapering from vent. The lateral line is distinct arched in the forward two fifths.
The scales are small.

Size —
Average weight 5 pounds; usually does not exceed 60 pounds.

Colour —
Colour is various shades of grey to green or brown to red depending on background, capable of changing to match surroundings. Back and sides have numerous rounded brownish to reddish spots; the lateral line is pale, fins are same tint as the body, the belly is whitish.

Old Chanty
"Cape Cod girls they have no combs,
They comb their hair with codfish bones.
Cape Cod boys they have no sleds,
They slide down dunes on codfish heads.
Cape Cod cats they have no tails,
They lost them all in sou'east gales."

Where Caught —
Codfish inhabit waters on both sides of the North Atlantic Ocean.
The principal fishing grounds of today are off Nova Scotia, Newfoundland, Greenland and Iceland.

How Processed —
Cod is used fresh, frozen, smoked, salted and canned. By-products include fish meal, cod liver oil and glue.
Split, salted & dried cod can be kept without spoiling for months, even in the tropics.

How Caught —
The Atlantic Cod is caught by Otter trawls, line trawls, hand lines, jiggers, pair trawls, Danish seines, traps and gill nets.

L.B. JENSON

Author's Note

Canada now is the world's largest exporter of fish. The centre of our fishing effort in the North West Atlantic lies in Nova Scotia. Strategically located near incredibly rich fishing grounds famous for five centuries, Nova Scotia's fishing industry is a source of great wealth and employment.

"Fishermen of Nova Scotia" is a collection of some of my previously published drawings together with many new ones. It is a picture story of our fisheries from the earliest discoveries to the present time. I have tried to show the variety of vessels, methods and gear used through the years and have illustrated variations used in different parts of the Province to meet special conditions. I am most grateful to the Minister of Fisheries for permission to reproduce in slightly altered form some of my illustrations for "Sea, Salt and Sweat".

When I first went to sea over forty years ago I was stirred by the sight of the great schooners on the Grand Banks, the sea alive with dories bobbing about and the dorymen hauling their trawls. I am happy that vessels and gear of those days have been lovingly preserved at the Fisheries Museum of the Atlantic in Lunenburg. "Fishermen of Nova Scotia" is a further tribute to our fishermen of yesterday and today. I also sincerely hope that this book will serve as an insite into Nova Scotia's most valuable and interesting industry, the inshore and offshore fisheries.

L. B. Jenson
Queensland,
R. R. 2 Hubbards,
Nova Scotia.

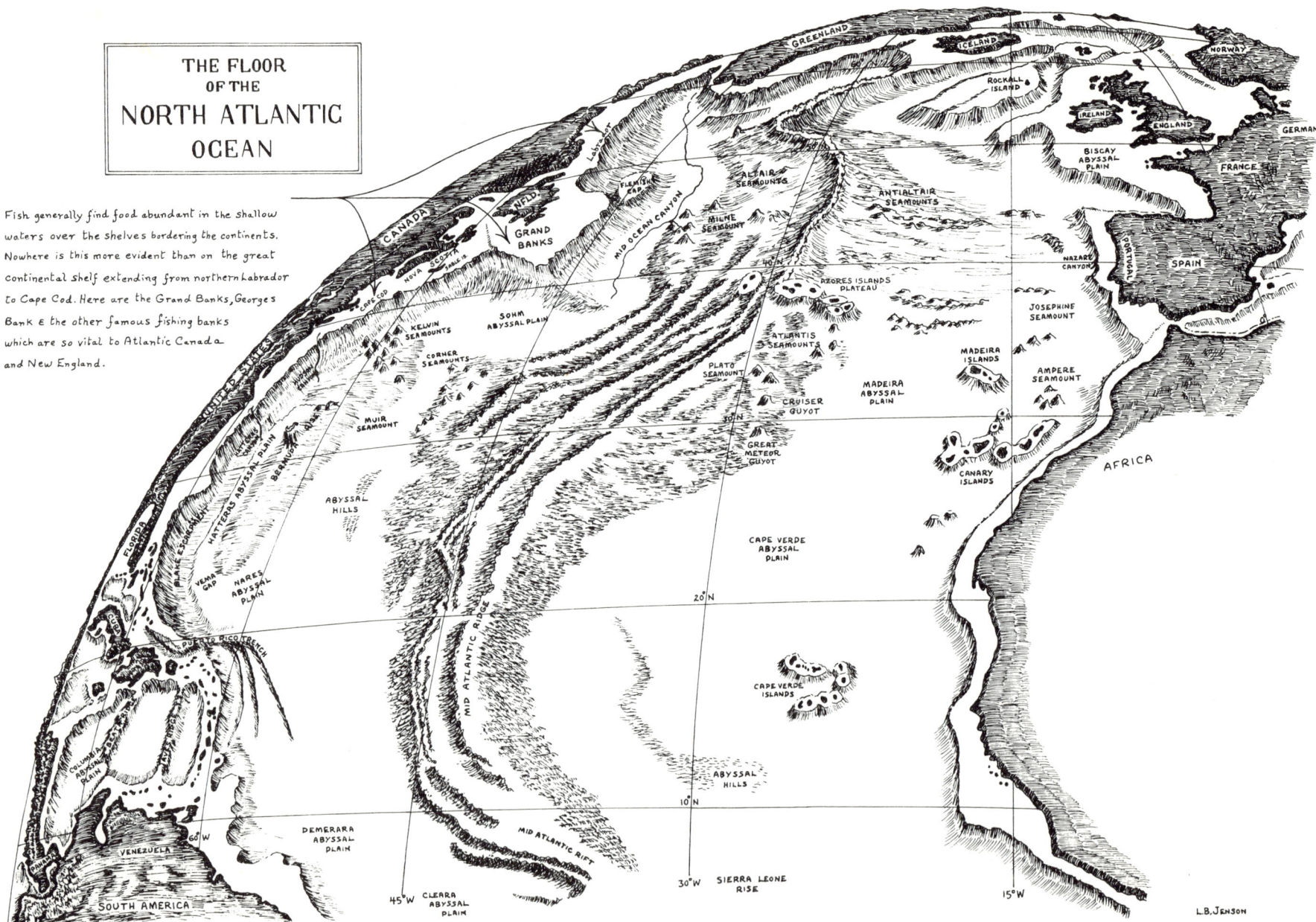

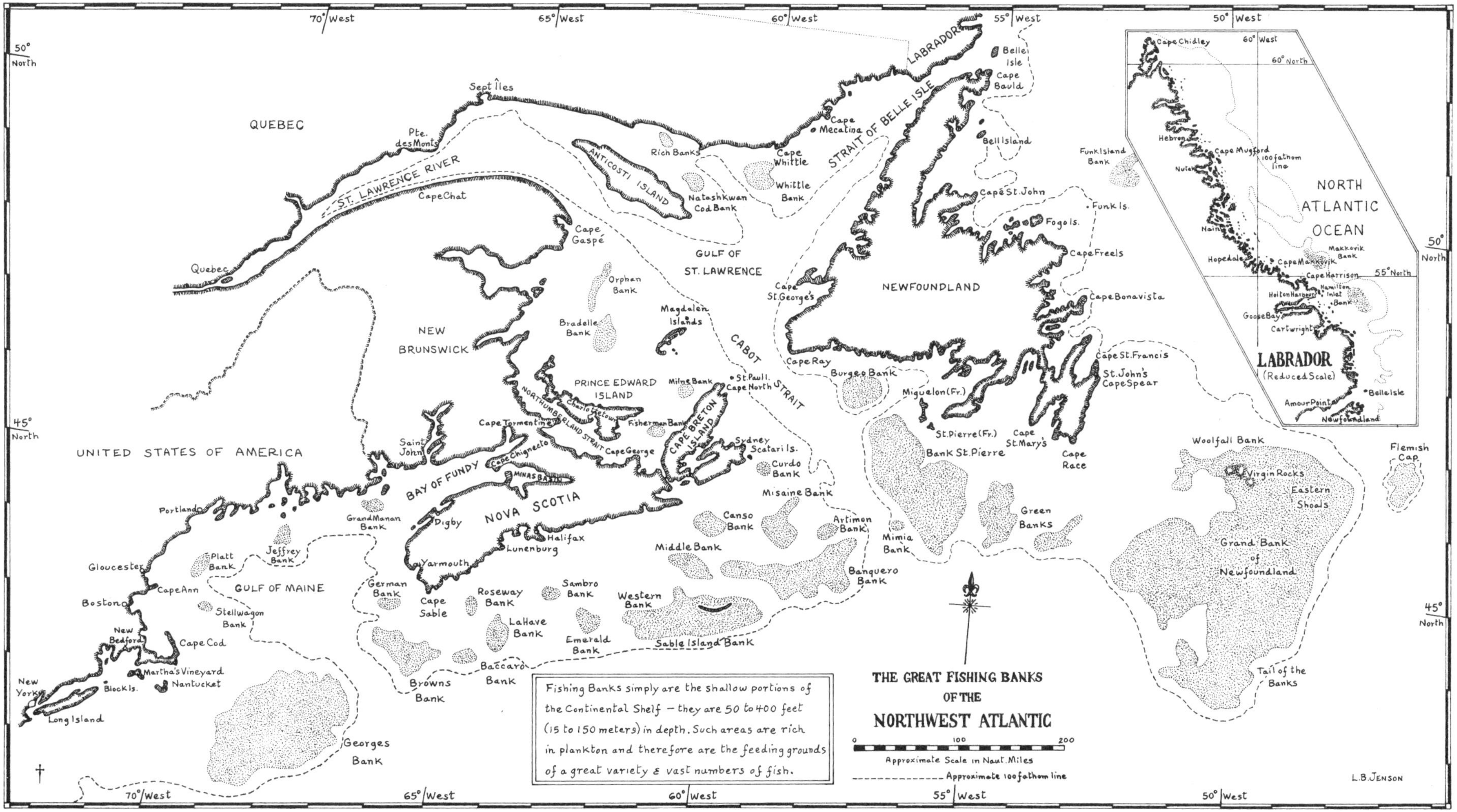

THE GREAT FISHING BANKS
OF THE
NORTHWEST ATLANTIC
Fishing Banks simply are the shallow portions of the Continental Shelf – they are 50 to 400 feet (15 to 150 meters) in depth. Such areas are rich in plankton and therefore are the feeding grounds of a great variety & vast numbers of fish.
Approximate Scale in Naut. Miles
0
100
200
Approximate 100 fathom line
L.B. JENSON
70° West
65° West
60° West
55° West
50° West
50° North
45° North
QUEBEC
Sept Îles
Pte. des Monts
ST. LAWRENCE RIVER
Cape Chat
Quebec
ANTICOSTI ISLAND
Rich Banks
Natashkwan Cod Bank
Cape Mecatina
Cape Whittle
Whittle Bank
LABRADOR
STRAIT OF BELLE ISLE
Belle Isle
Cape Bauld
Bell Island
Funk Island Bank
Cape St. John
Funk Is.
Fogo Is.
Cape Freels
Cape Bonavista
NEWFOUNDLAND
Cape St. George's
Cape Ray
Burgeo Bank
Miquelon (Fr.)
St. Pierre (Fr.)
Bank St. Pierre
Cape St. Mary's
Cape Race
Cape St. Francis
St. John's Cape Spear
GULF OF ST. LAWRENCE
Cape Gaspé
Orphan Bank
Bradelle Bank
Magdalen Islands
CABOT STRAIT
St. Paul I.
Cape North
Milne Bank
NEW BRUNSWICK
PRINCE EDWARD ISLAND
Charlottetown
NORTHUMBERLAND STRAIT
Cape Tormentine
Cape George
Fisherman Bank
CAPE BRETON ISLAND
Sydney
Scatari Is.
Curdo Bank
Misaine Bank
Canso Bank
Artimon Bank
Mimia Bank
Green Banks
Banquero Bank
Middle Bank
Saint John
Cape Chignecto
MINAS BASIN
BAY OF FUNDY
NOVA SCOTIA
Digby
Halifax
Lunenburg
Yarmouth
Grand Manan Bank
German Bank
Cape Sable
Roseway Bank
Sambro Bank
LaHave Bank
Emerald Bank
Western Bank
Sable Island Bank
Baccaro Bank
Browns Bank
UNITED STATES OF AMERICA
Portland
Gloucester
Cape Ann
Boston
Platt Bank
Jeffrey Bank
GULF OF MAINE
Stellwagon Bank
New Bedford
Cape Cod
Martha's Vineyard
Nantucket
Block Is.
New York
Long Island
Georges Bank
Woolfall Bank
Virgin Rocks
Eastern Shoals
Flemish Cap
Grand Bank of Newfoundland
Tail of the Banks
Cape Chidley
Hebron
Nutak
Cape Mugford
100 fathom line
Nain
Hopedale
Cape Makkovik
Makkovik Bank
Cape Harrison
Hamilton Inlet Bank
Goose Bay
Cartwright
NORTH ATLANTIC OCEAN
LABRADOR
(Reduced Scale)
Belle Isle
Amour Point
Newfoundland
60° West
60° North
55° North

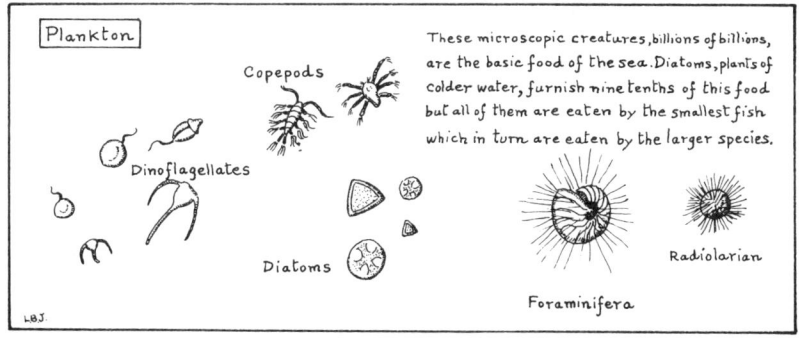

Plankton
These microscopic creatures, billions of billions, are the basic food of the sea. Diatoms, plants of colder water, furnish nine tenths of this food but all of them are eaten by the smallest fish which in turn are eaten by the larger species.
Copepods
Dinoflagellates
Diatoms
Radiolarian
Foraminifera
LBJ.

THE SEA FISHERIES OF NOVA SCOTIA
1978 CATCH

SUMMARY OF FISHING METHODS

Category	Species	Metric Tons	Value
PELAGIC & ESTUARIAL FISH — Pelagic fish are those living in zones between the surface & the sea bed. Estuarial fish are caught in or near river mouths. Catching methods are Purse Seine, Midwater Trawl, Floating Longline, Floating Gillnets, Automated Jigging, Inshore Trapnets and Weirs. Harpoons & Spears also are used.	HERRING	87,696 tons	$16 MILLION ($16,098,000)
	MACKEREL	8,675 tons	$1½ MILLION ($1,636,000)
	BLUEFIN TUNA	231 tons	$365,000
	ALEWIFE	4,285 tons	$688,000
	EEL	65 tons	$65,000
	SALMON	72 tons	$378,000
	SHAD	60 tons	$44,000
	SMELT	64 tons	$29,000
	OTHER PELAGIC	3,550 tons	$6 MILLION ($6,301,000)
GROUNDFISH or DEMERSAL FISH — These are found near or on the seabed. Catching methods are Bottom Trawl, Danish Seine, Gillnets, Longline and Pair Seine.	COD	79,634 tons	$25½ MILLION ($25,557,000)
	HADDOCK	40,435 tons	$18 MILLION ($17,851,000)
	REDFISH	21,525 tons	$4 MILLION ($4,212,000)
	HALIBUT	1,232 tons	$2½ MILLION ($2,548,000)
	SMALL FLATFISH	16,243 tons	$4½ MILLION ($4,430,000)
	GREENLAND TURBOT	1,141 tons	$208,000
	POLLOCK	26,857 tons	$5 MILLION ($5,050,000)
	WHITE HAKE	6,107 tons	$1½ MILLION ($1,418,000)
	CUSK	5,302 tons	$1½ MILLION ($1,424,000)
	CATFISH	1,416 tons	$256,000
	OTHER GROUNDFISH	3,829 tons	$531,000
MOLLUSC & CRUSTACEAN — Catching methods are Dredges (for Clams), Traps (for Crab & Lobster), Rakes (for Scallops), Weirs (for Eels), Nets (for Shrimp) & nearly all methods (for Squid).	CLAM	1,635 tons	$787,000
	MUSSEL	13 tons	$6,000
	OYSTER	107 tons	$76,000
	SCALLOP	106,235 tons	$62 MILLION ($61,744,000)
	SQUID	18,466 tons	$8 MILLION ($8,014,000)
	LOBSTER	6,161 tons	$30½ MILLION ($30,528,000)
	SNOW CRAB	3,095 tons	$2 MILLION ($1,916,000)
	OTHER CRAB	427 tons	$22,000
	SHRIMP	673 tons	$1½ MILLION ($1,340,000)
	OTHER MOLLUSC	27 tons	$10,000
MARINE PLANTS — Irish Moss, Kelp, Dulse & Rockweed. These are harvested by hand-raking, drag raking & shore raking.	MARINE PLANTS	19,899 tons	$2 MILLION ($1,856,000)
	OTHER PRODUCTS	81 tons	$19,000
	GRAND TOTAL VALUE		**$195½ MILLION ($195,508,000)**

L.B. JENSON

TRAWLING — Towing large nets behind fishing vessels.
  Bottom Trawl: towed nets with rollers which roll the nets over the seabed. An efficient method of fishing for cod.
  Semi-Pelagic Trawls: towed nets which skim over the seabed. Efficient for rough bottoms, fishing for cod, sandlaunce, squid, barracudina, argentines, silver hake & grenadiers.
  Midwater Trawls: towed nets which can be set at chosen depths. Efficient for redfish, herring, cod, capelin, dogfish, squid, cusk, silver hake, argentine & shrimp.

PURSE SEINING — Nets which encircle schools of fish. Efficient for tuna, and herring, mackerel, capelin & billfish. Compared with midwater trawls, purse seining cannot be fished in as rough weather, or in as great depths or in shoal water with a bad bottom.
  Powerblock Purse Seining: inshore & offshore, only 1 vessel & a power skiff.
  Ring Netting: inshore, requires 2 craft & much manual labour.
  Drum Seining: this is superseding powerblock seining. Cuts time by half & can be worked in slightly worse weather.

GILLNETTING — Drifting nets, or floating nets anchored, or sunken nets anchored. These entangle fish by their gills in the mesh. They are most beneficial in inshore vessels, especially those with low power, but can be used offshore with larger vessels. Can be efficient at catching almost any kind of fish, in particular where trawls & seines cannot be used. Gillnetting combines well with Longlining.

LONGLINING — A long line with hooks at intervals, the line either floating or sunk & anchored on the bottom. Much has been done to improve efficiency through mechanized & automated handling of the hooks, lines & baiting (Mustad system). This system eliminates the back-breaking, tiresome labour & sore hands of the old manual method. It is highly productive on grounds where trawlers cannot fish & where fish are too scattered for trawling. It can be used in any kind of weather, day or night.

JIGGING — Lines over the side are jigged up & down. Jigging is best suited to inshore craft & used for every species from codfish to squid. Automated jiggers are simple to fit & are relatively inexpensive.

TROLLING — Towing hooked lines. Used in Pacific but not in North Atlantic.

DANISH/SCOTTISH SEINING — Towing a net between 2 inshore craft. Efficient for Groundfish i.e. witch, flatfish, skate & Greenland halibut.

TRAPS — Trapping with pots for lobsters, crabs and eels. Inshore & offshore.

TRAPNETS — Inshore fishery: nets anchored near the shore.

SCALLOP RAKES — Large rakes towed over the seabed, used for scallops.

HARPOONS — Sometimes used for swordfish.

SPEARS — Sometimes used for eels.

DREDGES — Escalator type dredges are used for harvesting clams.

HANDLINING — Fishing over the side with a jigger, hooks & handline.

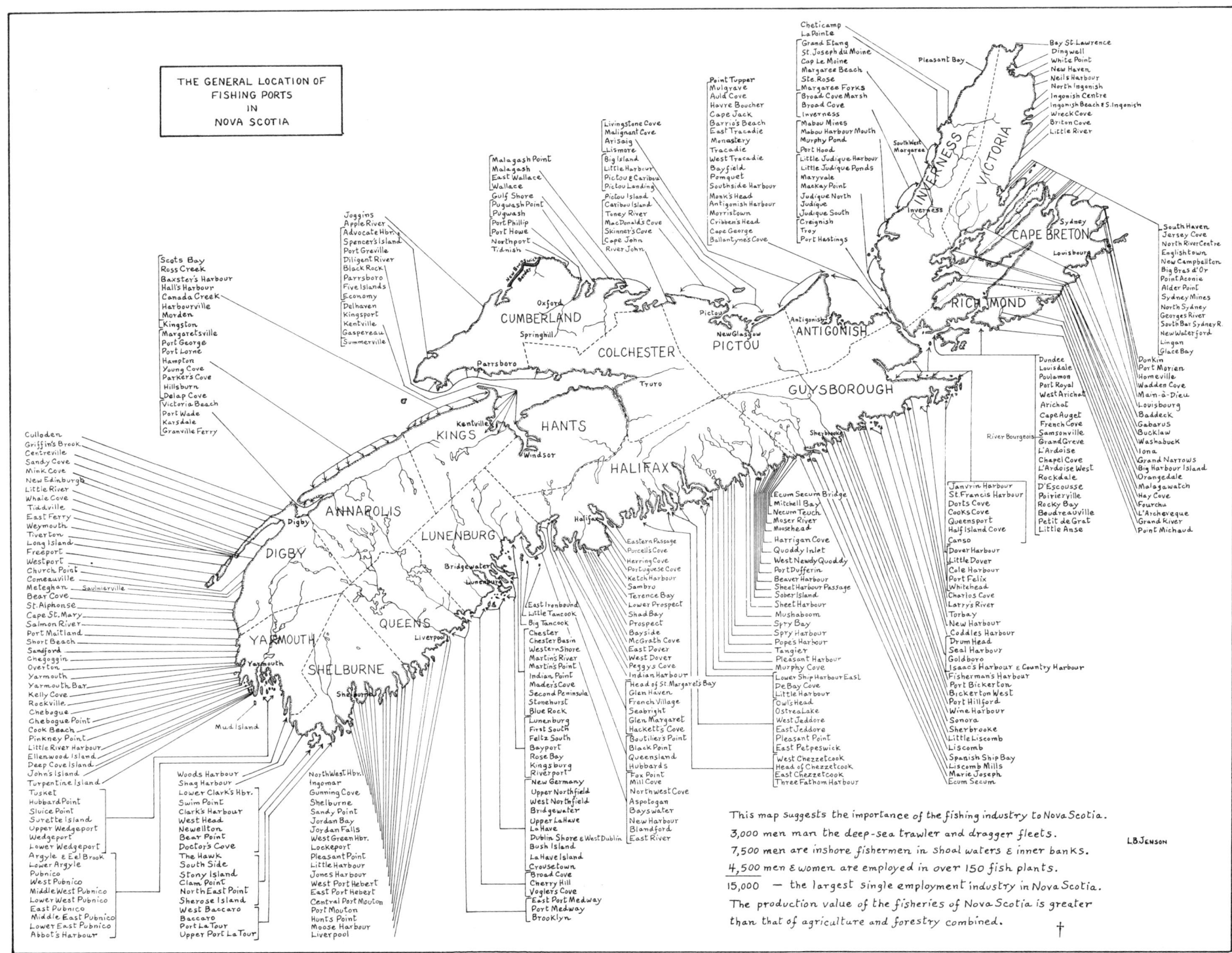

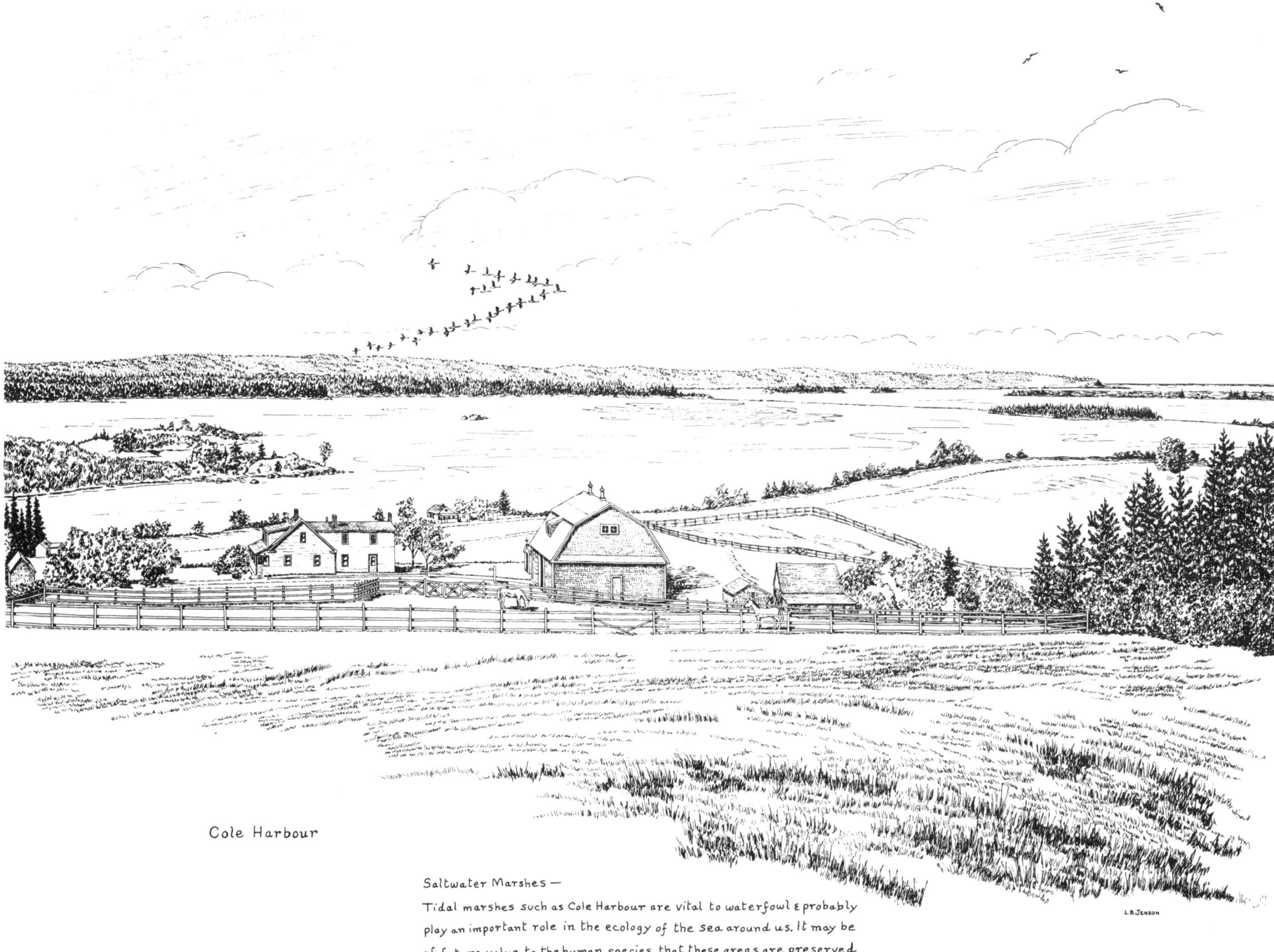

Cole Harbour

Saltwater Marshes —
Tidal marshes such as Cole Harbour are vital to waterfowl & probably play an important role in the ecology of the sea around us. It may be of future value to the human species that these areas are preserved in a pure & unaltered state, just as we would wish for our lakes & rivers.

Hubbards Cove — Fish Plant

Atlantic Sea Products Ltd. & Maxcatch Fisheries Ltd.

Over 150 local fish companies situated in the many harbours around the coast of Nova Scotia serve the fishermen of their particular area. Such firms buy fish from the local inshore fishermen & process them as fresh fillets, frozen blocks, salt fish dried in special chambers, smoked kippers etc. & also handle lobsters in season. Large firms run their own offshore fleets of trawlers and/or scallop draggers and thus catch, process & market their own fish. Selling is mostly by phone between the manager & the firm's agent in Toronto, Montreal, Boston or New York. Fish products are shipped by large, refrigerated tractor trailers direct from the plant to the market. Small independent fish firms such as the one shown above, employing local management & labour, are economic mainstays in our many little coastal communities.

MAP OF THE DISCOVERIES OF LABRADOR, NEWFOUNDLAND, CAPE BRETON & NOVA SCOTIA

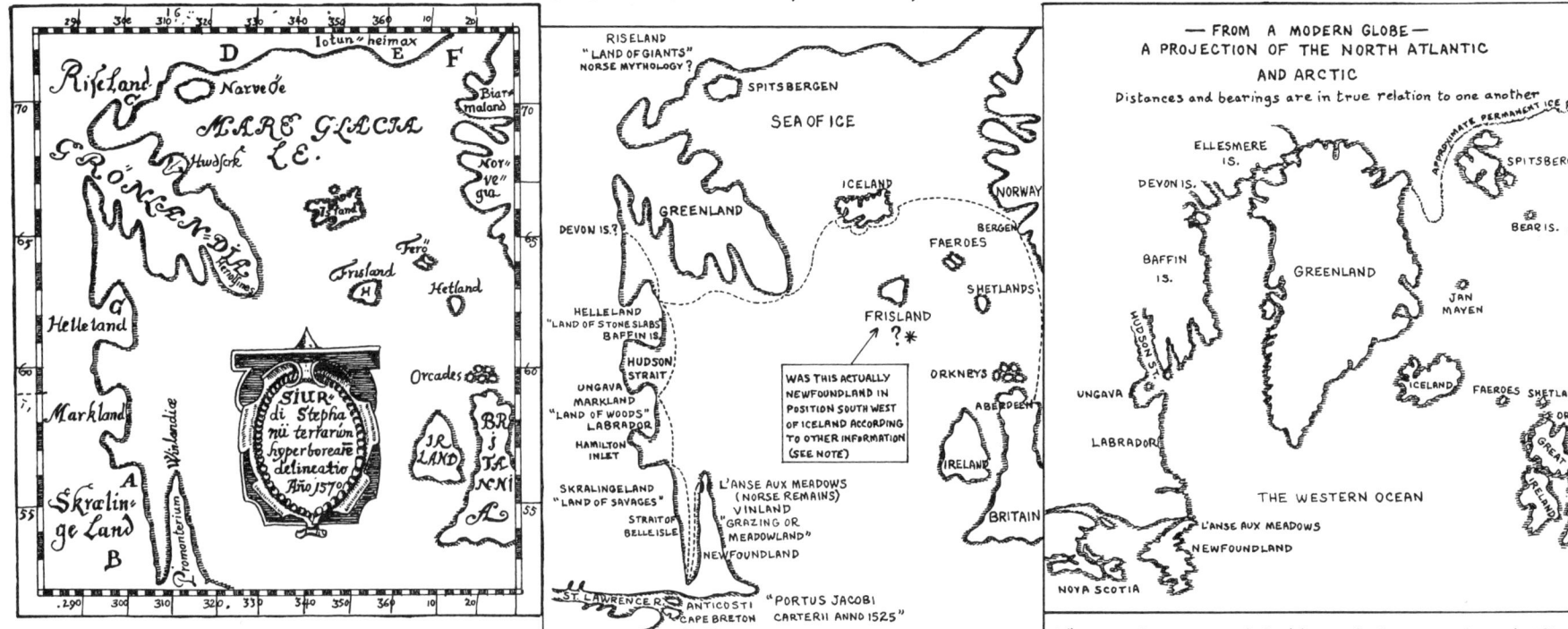

The Map by Sigurður Stéfansson of Iceland in 1570, a copy now in the Royal Library, Copenhagen, probably was based on earlier Icelandic maps. It is the first map we have which shows Vinland as described in Leif Eiriksson's saga in which he sailed from Greenland in 1,000 A.D. & discovered new lands to the Westward. The positive remains of a Norse settlement were uncovered in 1961 at L'Anse aux Meadows at the northern tip of Newfoundland. It is likely that the North Atlantic climate was relatively milder from about 900 A.D. to 1300 A.D. than it is at present.
L.B. JENSON

A Map similar to Stéfansson's and dated 1599 was found in Hungary after 1945. It shows the sailing routes to Vinland. A map by a Dane, Hans Resen, in 1605, showed Markland & Vinland in relation to Jacques Cartier's discoveries of the St. Lawrence River & is incorporated above. About 1410 Bristol men were fishing and trading in Icelandic & possibly Greenland waters, while about 1420 Basques were catching whales off Greenland and Labrador.

✳ "FRISLAND" was reported first by Nicolò Zeno I of Venice in 1390 as a possession of Henry Sinclair, Earl of Orkney. In 1659 Peter Heylyn's "Cosmography" described Frisland (from older documents) as lying south-west of Iceland, cold and barren, the inhabitants living mostly on and trading in fish. 'There is such abundance caught upon their coast that they are never without the company of Hanse-men, Scots, Hollanders, Danes and many English. The chief town is Freezland on the eastern shore. Westward is a lesser island Icaria.' Could Frisland have been Newfoundland & Cape Breton the lesser island. In any case "Frisland" did not appear on later maps.

Saint Brendon, an Irish monk, with fourteen companions set sail about 570 A.D. to cross the Atlantic in search of a "promised land". They certainly reached the West Indies, eastern North America and encountered the fog & icebergs of the North West Atlantic. Their vessel was the curragh, a wicker frame covered by leather — a type still in use in Ireland. It is light, strong and immensely seaworthy. It can be rowed or sailed.

Saint Brendon's Curragh c.570 A.D.

Leif Eiriksson's Knarr —
In the year 1001 A.D. Leif Eiriksson sailed from Greenland to Newfoundland and it is known that from then on several attempts were made by Norse people to settle in North America. The vessels used were not the romantic, fierce "dragon" ships, but round, wide trading ships called Knarrs built for cargoes or for carrying families with all their gear, horses and cattle. Norse ships were provisioned with dried cod.
A typical Knarr was about 52 feet long, beam 14 feet, and built of oak, pine & lime wood.

L.B. JENSON

The Yarmouth Runic Stone —
This 400 pound stone was found in 1790 by Dr. Fletcher near Overton. It may read "LAEIFR ERIKU RISR" (Leif to Erik raises this monument). At Tusket nearby there are supposed to be remains of Norse walls. Perhaps in time more substantial proof of Norse settlement will be found.

This illustration of St. Brendon is from a manuscript of the 1400's. The picture is fanciful but the vessel may be similar to that used by Prince Henry Sinclair of Orkney who probably sailed to Nova Scotia in 1394.

EARLY EXPLORERS OF THE NORTH ATLANTIC

NORSEMEN OF THE NORTH ATLANTIC

BASED ON SOME WOODCUTS BY OLAUS MAGNUS 1555

FAEROEMEN FLENSING A WHALE OF BLUBBER

ICELANDERS HARPOONING SEALS ON ICE FLOES

VIKINGS REPAIRING A BOAT

L.B. JENSON

A GREENLANDER IN A FIGHT WITH A SKRAELINGE

CATCHING, SMOKING AND DRYING SALMON IN THE SUN IN VINLAND

A Knarr, pre 1200.
This 50 foot vessel with its rope-strengthed square sail, was common in northern European waters.

A Cog
c.1242
This type of vessel was common in northern European waters from the 1200's to 1400's & would have been used for trade with Iceland. One ship such as this displaced 130 tons, was 77 feet long & had a beam of 24 feet. A Cog with its single square sail was managed with ease by a crew of 10. The rudder, slung at the centreline was a spectacular improvement over the heavy steering oar.

A Lateener — Transport for Crusaders
This 86 foot, two-decker with a crew of 30 carried 100 Crusaders from Italy to Asia Minor. Crusaders called them "Lateeners" after the Latin builders & crews & brought the idea to northern Europe.

DEVELOPEMENT OF TRANS-ATLANTIC SAILING CRAFT
1000 to 1500 AD

A Caravel
c.1490
The advantage of the lateen sails shown above, as opposed to square sails, is that a vessel so fitted is capable of leaving port with the wind blowing from almost any direction. Such a vessel also may be fitted with square fore & main sails when desired. This was the basic vessel of discovery used by the Portuguese & Spaniards in the 1400's & 1500's. A typical example of this was 70 feet long & had a crew of 25.

A "Hulk" of the Hanseatic League with a deck cargo of dried fish c. 1400's

In 1370 this type of vessel, a radical advance in the sail pattern up to that time, appeared. In the Mediterranean they were carvel-built (smooth hulls) and were known as "Carracks" while in Northern Waters they were clinker-built (planks overlap) and called "Hulks." Perhaps vessels similar to this fished the Grand Banks before the days of Columbus and Cabot. Dried salt cod kept easily & was a staple food for armies and winter provisions for all. It is interesting to note that "bonnets" (small sails lashed to the foot of the larger sail as shown) were still fitted in many Nova Scotian vessels within living memory.

L.B. JENSON

THE FIRST RECORDED VOYAGES

TO NORTHERN NORTH AMERICA

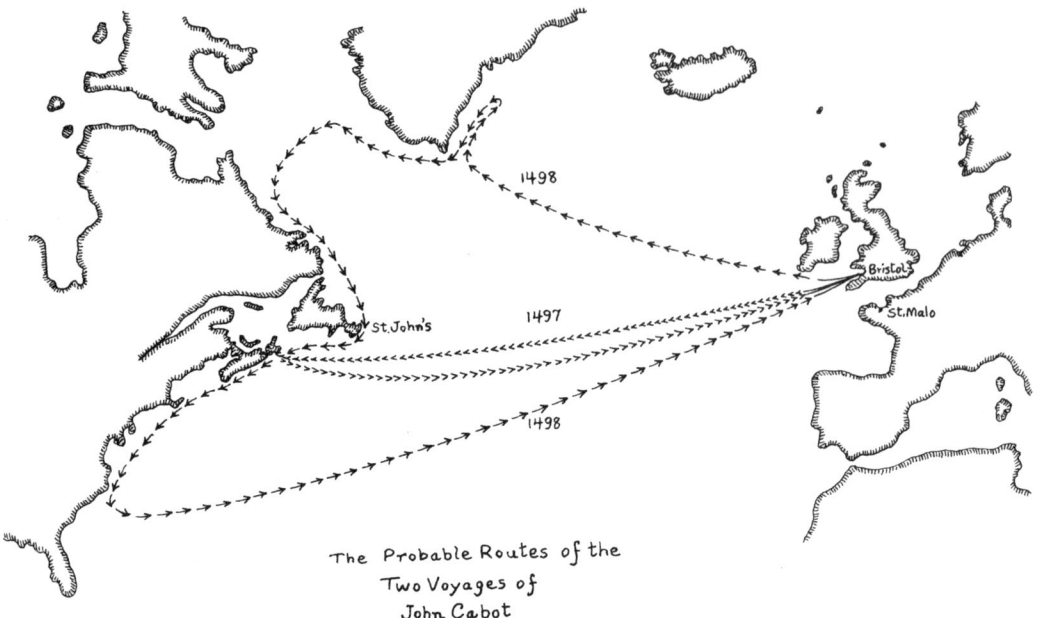

The Probable Routes of the Two Voyages of John Cabot

Instead of the spices, gold and other riches of Cathay, these brave men found and reported the vast numbers of the humble cod fish on the Great Banks of Newfoundland, which turned into greater riches than they could imagine and still are and will continue to be, if properly managed, a constant living resource of true riches to the world. Even as I glance up from this sketch, I can see from my window fishermen sailing for the Banks for the mighty cod — and bringing back money & employment to our small village.

L.B. JENSON ©

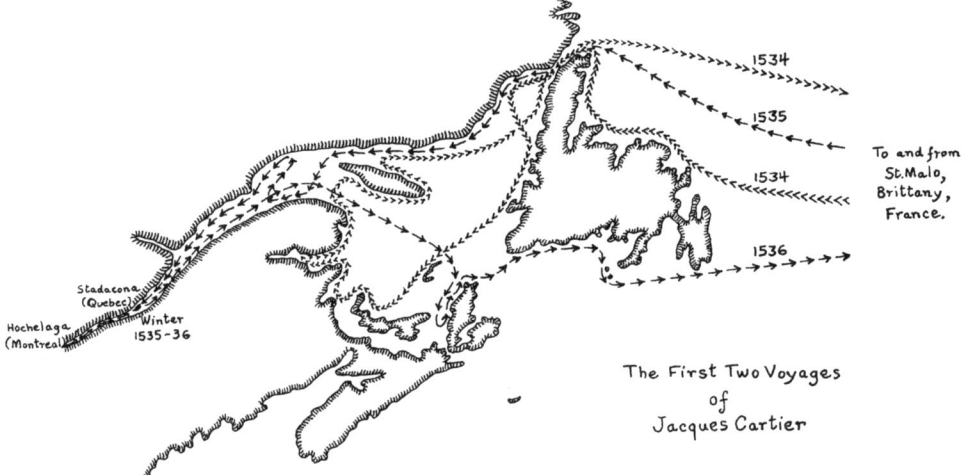

The First Two Voyages of Jacques Cartier

John Cabot's Navicula
"Mathew"
—1497—

L.B. Jenson
(after a model in Bristol)

Even before Columbus rediscovered America, merchants in the English port of Bristol had sent out vessels to probe the Atlantic for "Brasil", one of the islands of legend & possible trading interest. When the Italian navigator John Cabot came to Bristol in the 1490's he found merchants eager to support his plan to sail westward to Cathay by a northern route. He was given letters patent by King Henry VII approving his plan and sailed in May 1497 with about 20 men in the bark Mathew, capacity 50 tons. On 24 June, 1497, they found land & named it "Newfoundland". They went back to Bristol & returned in 1498. Although they did not find the spices & riches they sought, they brought back news of the great fishing wealth of the region. As fish was a vital item of food, soon fishermen from Europe set out for the shoals of cod on the great Banks. Cabot's explorations established English claims to North America.

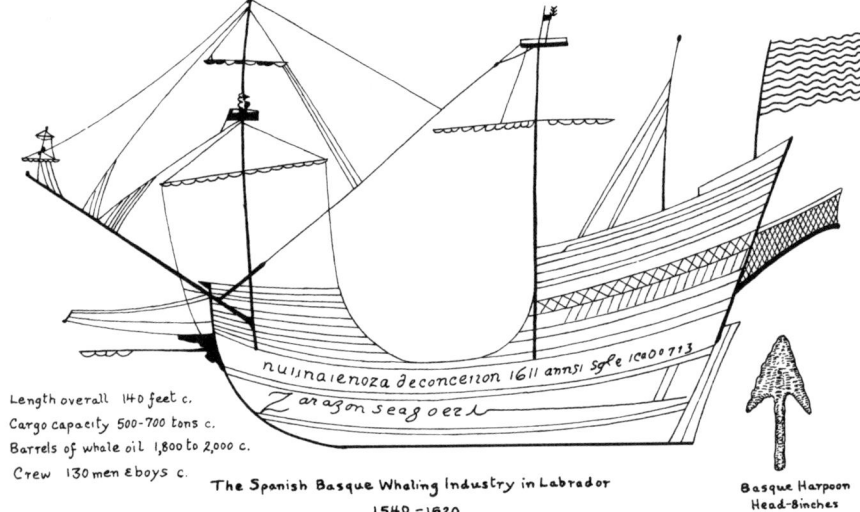

Length overall 140 feet c.
Cargo capacity 500-700 tons c.
Barrels of whale oil 1,800 to 2,000 c.
Crew 130 men & boys c.

Basque Harpoon
Head-8inches

The Spanish Basque Whaling Industry in Labrador
1540-1620

The above sketch is based on a recently discovered contemporary drawing of a Spanish galleon, 1611. Vessels similar to this sailed from north-east Spain to the Labrador coast of the Gulf of St. Lawrence for the whaling industry. Whales were hunted from shallops and their oil rendered down in shore ovens. It was carried back to Europe in barrels aboard the galleons. Of course English, Breton, Spanish and the Portuguese were fishing the Banks for cod fish from 1500 onwards.

L.B. JENSON

COD FISHING IN THE NEW FOUND BANKS
Circa 1500's

L.B.J.

A European Cod Fisherman in North America before permanent settlement. (based on an old print). His clothing is made of oiled skins.

A North American Fishing Station before permanent European settlement — here were sheds & stages for cleaning, salting & sun-drying catches, nearby there probably was a vegetable garden for fresh provisions. Note the pre-fabricated boat assembled at the station.

L.B. JENSON (from an old print)

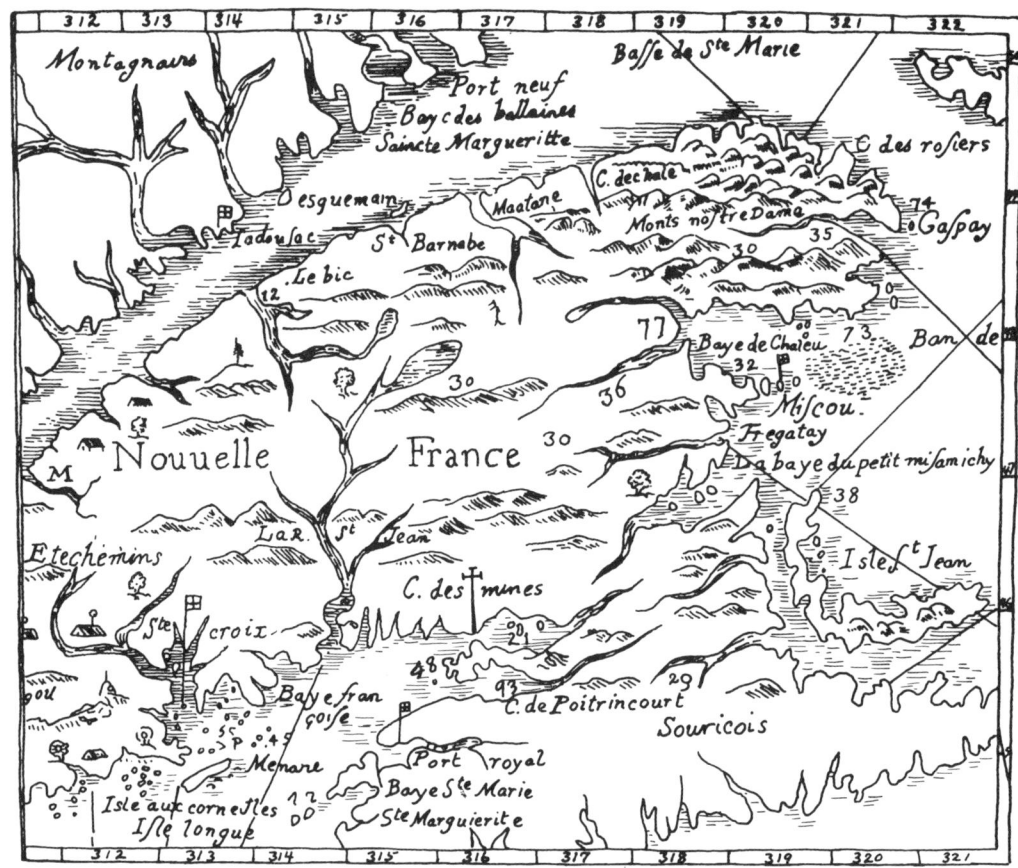

Champlain's General Map of the Maritimes (a tracing)

In 1604 Champlain began to chart the various places which he explored. This map, crude as it may seem to our eyes, together with two other general maps, plus over a dozen charts of important harbours, represent the most advanced cartographic achievement up to that time. It is impossible for anyone to imagine the difficulties of mapping new country accurately. It is surprising how deceptive an appearance a country presents; hills obscure one's vision, peninsulas may appear as islands, a varied coast appears straight in haze and so on. These daunting problems faced Champlain in his charting forays along the coast, mostly in a bobbing open boat, such as the shallop shown above on the right.

A Shallop - circa 1600
(Traced from Champlain's engraving in "Les Voyages" of 1613)
A Shallop primarily was a rowing boat, small enough to be carried on the deck of a transatlantic ship or to be towed across. She had one or two masts, square-rigged or lateen. The shallop was the work boat for fishermen or fur traders.

SAMUEL CHAMPLAIN
FATHER OF NEW FRANCE, ONE OF THE GREATEST PIONEERS, EXPLORERS AND COLONISTS OF ALL TIME.

1570 - Born at Brouge.
1599-1601 - to Spain & West Indies.
1603 - First voyage to Canada, to site of Montreal and return.
1604 - Voyage to L'Acadie, Bay of Fundy and New England. Port Royal founded.
1607 - Returns to France.
1608-09 - To Canada, founds Quebec.
1610 - Canada & return to France
1611 - Canada & return to France etc. etc.

In total, including three round voyages to the West Indies, Champlain crossed the Atlantic 29 times (23 between France and Canada)

1635 - Died at Quebec.

L. B. JENSON

L.B. JENSON   1534 – JACQUES CARTIER'S VESSEL "GRANDE HERMINE" 100 TONS OF St MALO

In 1534 King Francis I of France commissioned Jacques Cartier of St. Malo to make a voyage to the new found lands to "discover certain islands and countries where it is said there will be found great quantities of gold and other riches." At 42 Cartier probably had several American voyages to his credit. He noted much fishing and even met a large vessel from La Rochelle. In his voyages he visited the sites of Quebec City and Montreal. In general he pioneered methods of surviving the Canadian winter and gave Europe more information of the land now forming eastern Canada. †

"Don de Dieu" 1608 – one of Samuel Champlain's ships.
With this and other vessels Champlain carried the first permanent French settlers to Canada.

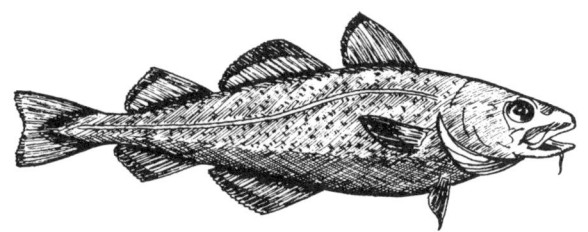

CATCHING, CLEANING AND PRESERVING CODFISH

The Historic Importance of Codfish. It was not the fur trade or precious metals which drew our first colonists, but cod! Dried and salted cod fed the European armies of the Middle Ages. Before refrigeration, cod was one of the few protein foods in the world which could be preserved almost indefinitely, even in hot, moist climates. The development of the great cod fisheries of the North West Atlantic from the time of Cabot necessitated settlements where the fish could be dried; hence the first colonization of North America.

Description. Cod are ground fish of an average weight of 5 pounds. The record size is 200 pounds, but over 60 pounds is relatively rare. Codfish are voracious bottom feeders and range in vast numbers on the shallow portions of the continental shelf at depths of 50 to 400 feet. When hooked, these fish are left limp and without fight from the long haul from the bottom to the surface.

Processing As soon as possible after being caught, the fish were dressed. Trestle tables called "Keelers" were set up on deck, and dressing crews got to work. The <u>Throater</u> cut out the tongues which he dropped in a bucket, then he snapped off the fish heads. The <u>Gutter</u> disembowelled the fish, put the liver in the liver butt (a tub) and threw the entrails over the side. (In harbour, entrails were tossed in the "Gurry Kid"). The <u>Splitter</u> cut the fish down the middle, cut away the backbone, flattened the fish and dropped it into a tub of salt water to soak clean. The fish were then piled and packed in the hold by the <u>Salters</u>. Each layer of fish was covered with generous scoops of salt. Baskets of salt were brought by the <u>Salters' Devils</u>, often boys. In this manner the catch was preserved in the hold of the vessel for 2 or 3 months until it could be landed.

Curing Once the catch was landed, the split and salted fish were spread to dry in the sun and wind for four or five days. The fish had to be turned frequently and at the first sign of rain or fog they had to be gathered and placed under cover. A "soft cure" was after only a day or two in the sun and resulted in "wet fish."

The Final Product — A Salt Cod

Cod Flakes For the purpose of curing the fish, cod flakes were used. These were long, narrow, wooden platforms on posts about three feet off the ground. Until the 1950's, cod flakes were a common sight around the coastal villages in Nova Scotia, indeed in all the Maritimes.

Fresh Fishing. For the fresh fish market, the dressed fish were stowed in layers of shaved ice. The fish had to be landed within ten days to prevent spoiling.

Haddock — up to 10 pounds but average 2 to 4 pounds

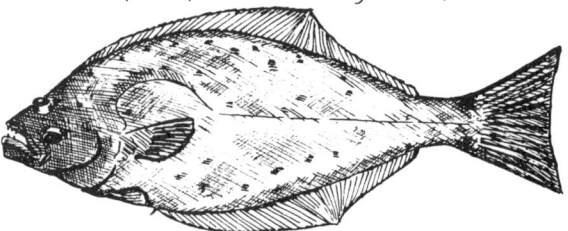

Atlantic Halibut — record 700 pounds, average 50 pounds

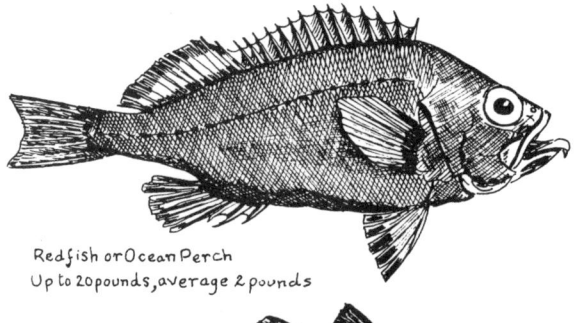

Redfish or Ocean Perch
Up to 20 pounds, average 2 pounds

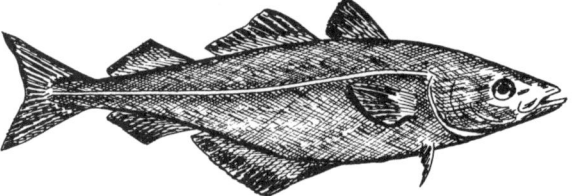

Pollock — up to 60 pounds, but average 5 to 10 pounds

OTHER COMMERCIAL FISHES OF THE BANKS

L.B. JENSON

The Reason for Schooners

"'Tis the frost that makes coasting navigation so difficult and almost impractical to ships. The running ropes freeze in the blocks; the sails are stiff like sheets of tin; and the men cannot expose their hands long enough to the cold to do their duty aloft; so that the topsails are not easily handled, however sloops and schooners where the men stand on deck and do all their work, succeed well enough."

Admiral Colville to the Admirality
Halifax, Nova Scotia; April 1761.

The Marblehead Schooner or "Heel Tapper"

These Schooners were being built and sailed in Nova Scotian waters in the 1750's. They were about 50 feet long with a beam of 18 feet and drew 6 feet. They were developed from the American Chesapeake Schooner and used for offshore fishing, trading & even as war vessels with 8 ten-pounder guns. When used for fishing, it was by handlining from the deck. Sometimes they were called "Heel Tappers" because of the shoe-like appearance of the hull. †

L.B. JENSON

**Fish Stores and Cod Drying on Fish Flakes
Lunenburg Harbour in the 1930's**

This method of preserving fish was used for centuries and it was only in the late 1940's that the back-breaking labour of laying out the fish, turning them, bringing them in from the rain and laying them out again, was replaced by modern drying ovens. †

A Dogger
† A two-masted, ketch-like fishing smack, broad in the beam & with a fish well in the centre, used in the German ocean (North Sea) — Vessels such as these also were used by both England & France on the Banks of the North West Atlantic.

May, 1776

Towards the middle of May we approached the Banks of Newfoundland, which are a surprising range of sunken mountains, extending in a direct line not less than three hundred and thirty miles in length, and about seventy five in breadth. The top of the ridge, which at its highest reaches within five fathoms of the water's surface, is frequented by vast multitudes of lesser fish on which the excellent cod feeds, fattens, and multiplies in inconceivable quantities. Though hundreds of vessels have been laden for centuries past from thence, no scarcity or decrease of cod happens.

During the greater part of our passage across the Banks we never saw the sun, owing to the thick, hazy atmosphere which prevails in that part of the ocean. For two days together a total darkness like midnight covered the sky, so that a continuous firing of guns and beating of drums was needed to enable the ships of the convoy to keep due distance and avoid fouling one another. There also was the danger of running down fishing-vessels, from whose unseen decks hoarse shouts of warning against collision frequently arose. In spite of such risks it was customary for convoys to travel along a depression in the middle of the Banks, which was named the Ditch. The water here was as calm as in a bay, though the winds on either side were extremely impetuous.

At last came a stiff wind and with it a break in the fog. We saw the disc of the sun, dim and red, but gradually blazing with what seemed to us more than its usual splendour. In the welcome light we observed how numerous a congregation of fishing-vessels, large and small, lay about us. In times of peace, we were told, more than three thousand sail were annually to be counted there. A vast flock of sea-fowl was in attendance on the vessels, wheeling above them and ever and again swooping down to the decks to snatch up a cod's head or some other fishy prize. Besides the familiar gulls and many larger birds of the same feather, we observed a flightless, swimming, knowing sort, called penguins. They were sporting in pairs here and there, and ducking deep down in the water in chase of fish. Here the sea was no longer of the usual azure blue, but of a sandy white colour. We were now permitted to supplement our diet of salt meat and maggotty biscuit with fresh-caught cod. We baited a hook first with the entrails of a fowl and soon pulled up a fish. The hook was then baited with the entrails of this fish, which was gutted in its turn, and presently we were hauling in cod as fast as one can imagine. The water magnified the size of them so that it seemed almost impossible to get them aboard, and their struggles were very obdurate.

May, 1776

The right of fishing on these Banks, though by the law of nature it should have been common to all nations, had been appropriated by the French and British, who at this time had frigates constantly cruising to prevent encroachment by ships of other nations. And, by an Act of the previous year, the revolted colonists of New England had been excluded from the Banks, though it was on the cod-fishery that their wealth had been founded and was still largely maintained. The New Englanders took this very hard, and the fishermen of Marblehead and Salem who lost their employment because of the Act were, as privateers, to do us more mischief in the war almost than any other class of Americans.

We passed close by several of these fishing-vessels, which had galleries erected on the outside of the rigging from the mainmast to the stern, and sometimes the whole length of the ship. On the galleries were ranged barrels with the tops struck out, into which the fishermen would get to shelter themselves from the weather. The stay of these vessels on the Banks was but short, for the method of curing was as quick as the catching. As soon as the cod was hauled up, the fisherman cut out its tongue, then passed it to a mate who struck off its head, plucked out liver and entrails, and tossed it to a third hand, who drew out the bone as far as the navel, then down the carcass went into the hold. In the hold stood men who salted and ranged the cod-fish in exact piles, taking care that just sufficient salt was laid between each two rows of fish to prevent them from touching.

It was on this sunny day, May 14th, that we first saw icebergs; but these were small bergs floated down from the St. Lawrence River. Four days later we had a view of the mountains of Newfoundland, covered with snow. We had been forty days at sea without landfall and this dreary island was therefore very pleasant to our eyes.

Roger Lamb

The Banks of Newfoundland, 14th May, 1776.
Extracts from the Journal of Sergeant Roger Lamb of the British Army, who fought in the American Revolution. The above describes a part of the passage from Cork, Ireland, to Quebec in the Transport "Friendship". The "penguin" described was the Great Auk, now sadly extinct.
The Journal was published by Robert Graves in 1940 as "Sergeant Lamb's America". It is an intensely interesting study of a British view of the American Revolution.

L.B. JENSON

St. Andrew's Presbyterian Church
Lunenburg, Nova Scotia.
Opened for worship 3rd July, 1770.

The oldest Presbyterian Church in Canada is crowned by a weathervane of a codfish of pure copper, 5½ feet long, atop a spire 160 feet high. It serves as a reminder of the fishing industry that has supported Lunenburg for over two centuries. Also the fish was the secret symbol of the first Christians. The initial letters of the Greek words for "Jesus Christ, God's Son, Savior" spell the Greek word for "fish". ΙΧΘΥΣ

St. John's Anglican Church — Lunenburg
Erected in 1753 at the founding of this old fishing town
In the early 1900's when the salt banking trade was in it's heyday, 10th March probably was the most propitious day on the deepsea fisherman's calendar. If the weather was favourable, ideally a westerly breeze, there was the great exodus from Lunenburg for the "frozen baiting" trip & forty or so vessels spread their great sails for the Banks. Many a lad of 9 or 10 set off on his first trip that day. On the Sunday before sailing, families would attend Church service — a special occasion when their sons were about to leave their childhood astern and sail into their manhood in a dangerous and exacting occupation.

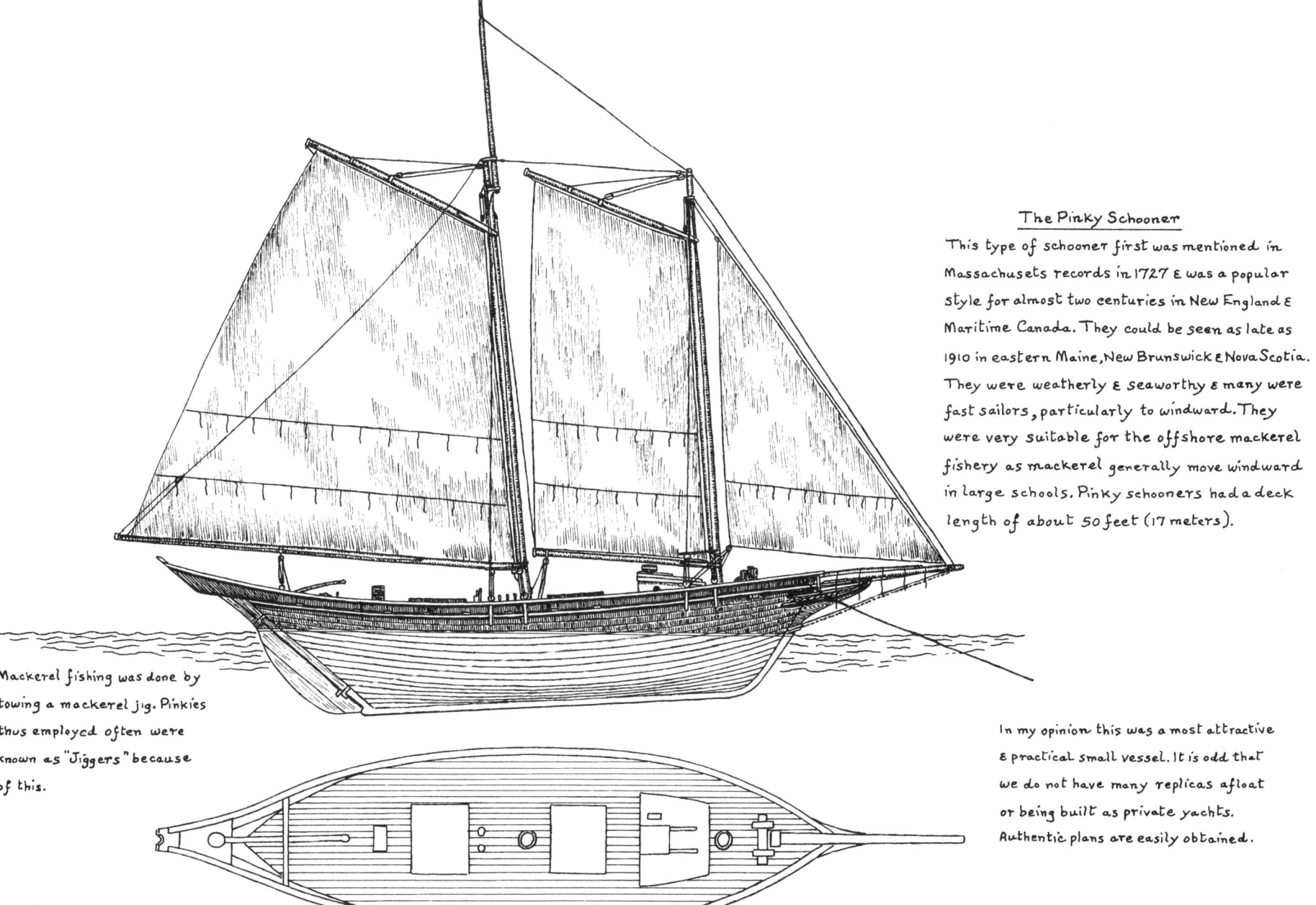

The Pinky Schooner

This type of schooner first was mentioned in Massachusets records in 1727 & was a popular style for almost two centuries in New England & Maritime Canada. They could be seen as late as 1910 in eastern Maine, New Brunswick & Nova Scotia. They were weatherly & seaworthy & many were fast sailors, particularly to windward. They were very suitable for the offshore mackerel fishery as mackerel generally move windward in large schools. Pinky schooners had a deck length of about 50 feet (17 meters).

Mackerel fishing was done by towing a mackerel jig. Pinkies thus employed often were known as "Jiggers" because of this.

In my opinion this was a most attractive & practical small vessel. It is odd that we do not have many replicas afloat or being built as private yachts. Authentic plans are easily obtained.

L.B. JENSON

A Chebacco Boat — Dogbody Type
(a large Shallop)
Used in Nova Scotia in the early 1800's †

THE NOVA SCOTIAN PRIVATEER "LIVERPOOL PACKET" 1811-1815

ex "Black Joke", a Slave Tender captured by the Royal Navy and auctioned as a prize by Vice Admiralty Court in Halifax in 1811 at the Rooms of the Spread Eagle for £440 to Enos Collins of Halifax and Benjamin Knaut & John and James Barss of Liverpool. She was a Baltimore Clipper Schooner LOA 53 feet, beam 19 feet, hold depth 6½ feet. Tons displacement 67. Fumigated with tar, vinegar & brimstone. Armed at His Majesty's Dockyard, Halifax with one 6 pounder gun, 4-12 pounder guns, pistols, muskets, pikes, cutlasses, grappling irons and nets. Later, captured great spruce oars for rowing out of danger in calms. Crew of 40 men from Nova Scotia. Captain Joseph Barss of Liverpool. Prizes captured off New England during War of 1812 to 1814 between Great Britain & United States of America totalled over a quarter of a million dollars. Captured herself on 11 June, 1812, off Portsmouth, New Hampshire, by American Privateer "Thomas" & crew jailed. Sold & renamed "Portsmouth Packet", Captain John Perkins. Captured off Mount Desert Island by H.M.S. "Fantome" & sold in Halifax to firm of Collins & Allison. Renamed "Liverpool Packet." Under Captain Caleb Seely of Saint John, New Brunswick, & then Captain Knaut of Liverpool, she sailed successfully, capturing her last prize in December, 1814, the end of that War.

A Clipper Schooner †
—1867—

Hand-lining on the Banks
circa 1830
(after old prints) †

L.B. JENSON

Hard work on Georges Bank —
Hand lining from a schooner's deck
in the 1850's. (after an old print) †

A Tancook Whaler
1860 to the present †

A Nova Scotian Pinky Schooner
— 1875 —

A Tancook Fisherman's Year

Note —
Whalers had to be moored offshore and fish were forked into dories which were rowed ashore. Dories were hauled up by hand winch or oxen to the dressing tables for salting down. Women and children helped.

Spring Mackerel were not as good as in the Fall. The spring catch was sold to the West Indies. The fall catch was sold to the Americans.

Dec. & Jan. — Lobstering around the Tancooks and islands & ledges of Mahone Bay.

Feb. & March — Make and mend gear.

March & April — Lobstering.

May — For 3 or 4 weeks set nets for the spring Mackerel run.

June, July & Aug. — Fish for Cod, Haddock and Pollock by handlining and sometimes, setting trawls.
Squid was the best bait but Herring was used most frequently.
On the first day nets were set for Herring bait. On the second & third days, handlining took place.
Fish & potatoes (cooked on a small stove) and bread with molasses were the main diet.

Fall Season — Make hay for cattle. Some vessels went to Cape Breton for Swordfish and brought back coal. Swordfish were dressed, iced & sold in Cape Breton for Boston.

September — Herring netted for West Indian market. Herring are the most delicate fish & had to be dressed and salted down as soon as possible.

Oct. and Nov. — Made Sauerkraut. Dried Cod. Sailed loads of cabbages to Halifax.

Nov. and Dec. — Scalloping in Mahone Bay (using special transom-sterned boats) Duck hunting along the shore.

L. B. JENSON

THE TANCOOK WHALER
An INSHORE FISHERMAN, first 24 to 28 feet, by 1900 - 50 feet.

Developed about 1860 by the Mason, Langille & Stevens families of Big Tancook & Little Tancook Islands in Mahone Bay near Lunenburg. Their main fishing trips were in summer, two three day trips a week to their grounds, 18 miles South-east of Cross Island Light. They left Monday AM, home Wednesday to land their catch, out again & back on Saturday. They became rare about 1910.

from photograph in Lunenburg Harbour, June 1932, courtesy Nova Scotia Museum.

The design is thought to be evolved from the whaleboats used by whaling vessels and in a way it resembles the Viking Longships. The Tancook Islands have no natural harbours and the vessels had to be moored off the land facing the frequently severe weather all the year long. The prolonged morning calms often made it necessary for the men to row long distances towards their fishing grounds. The best groundfish area was about 35 miles off.

Tancook Whalers were "double-enders", remarkably sharp in their lines, carvel built (i.e. smooth hulled), sat low in the water with a very graceful sheer, had an outside rudder, raking stern post and a bald clipper bow. They were ballasted with beach stones and the ballast had to be shifted each time the whaler came about. They carried two 14 foot oars and rowlocks. They were fast sailers. Early in the 1900's engines were fitted.

Necessity Breeds Ingenuity

The Tancook Whaler is an excellent example of a design adapted to meet special local conditions. In this case, complicated machinery dependent on imported fuels, freezing and cold storage facilities, rapid transportation to distant markets etc. did not exist.

This was the general state in Nova Scotia 100 years ago. However with hard work and great ingenuity people prospered in the fisheries. Such conditions still exist in many countries today and one might wonder if it is wise to introduce our modern fishing methods in such places and change the traditional methods before proper shore complexes, paved roads and all our other social facilities exist.

The Schooner "America" 1851

LB JENSON

The sailing qualities & speed of the North American schooners prompted the building of a number for wealthy sportsmen for ocean racing. The most famous of the was the "America". ‡

— Shallop — 
A handliner of 1770 †

L.B. JENSON
(from a photo courtesy Maritime Museum of the Atlantic)

SHAD-FISHING BOATS — PARRSBORO SHORE, NOVA SCOTIA
1893

American Shad (Herring Family)

American Shad is the aristocrat of the Herring Family. A large, tasty fish it is on average 2 feet long & about 4 pounds weight. They live in coastal waters & ascend rivers to spawn each spring (after the Alewives). At one time Shad were abundant & of commercial importance all along the Atlantic coast but pollution in rivers & streams has reduced the catch by 80%!

In 1900 there were 60 to 80 boats similar to those shown above which were shad fishing by Drift Net in Coboquid Bay. These 25 foot boats are uniquely designed for this Bay which, being an extension of the Bay of Fundy, dries for miles at low tide. They have a centreboard & the plank bottom allows them to sit on the mud.

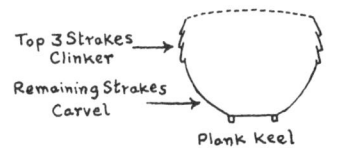

Beam Section — Shad-Fishing Boat

Top 3 Strokes Clinker
Remaining Strokes Carvel
Plank Keel

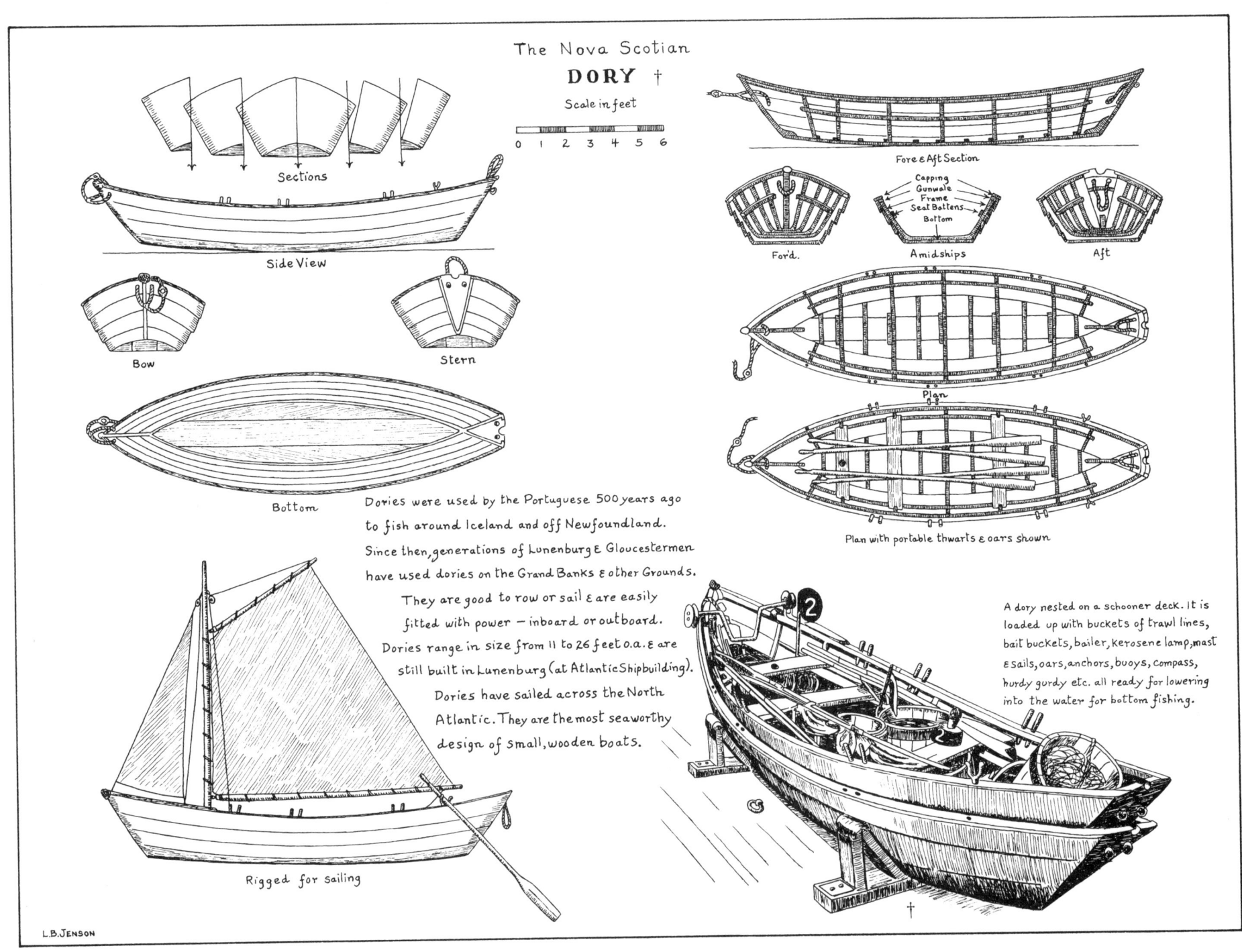

FISHING FROM BANKS SCHOONERS
1700's to 1963

IN THE BEGINNING — HANDLINING

From the schooner deck — This was the original method of fishing. The desired depth was 50 to 100 feet. Each line was weighted with a 3 to 5 pound lead sinker & fitted with 2 hooks baited with shucked clams or one inch squares of herring or mackerel.

Handlining from dories — In the early 1800's American schooners began to carry dories to the Banks. One or two men each, in a number of dories, could cover a greater area of bottom than the same number of men in one vessel. 6 or 7 lines were put over from each dory.

TRAWL FISHING

About 1850 began the heroic, dangerous & extremely profitable Trawl Method, the practice of laying & hauling trawls from dories. This practice prevailed for over a century, until 1963 when "Theresa E. Connor" could no longer recruit dorymen.

Dories and their Equipment

Schooners carried 6 to 12 dories nested on the deck. They were painted yellow-orange or buff for maximum visibility in fog, snow or dusk. Dory equipment was: a jug of water, food, 4 oars, mast & sail, two 17 pound kedge anchors, 2 or 3 buoys (small kegs) & markers, 2 to 4 trawl tubs, thwarts, pen boards, bailers, kerosene flare, gaff, club, gurdy, bait tub & dory compass. All gear was marked with the number of the dory. The plug was secured with a loop inboard & a loop on the flat bottom outboard, a handhold in case of capsizing. A dory could hold about 1,700 pounds of fish. A dory heaped with fish & low in the water marked a "high liner."

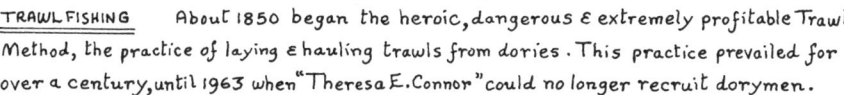

The Trawl The trawl was a stout, hard-laid, tarred cotton ground line a mile or more long. Every 3 feet or so a "snood" or "gangen" — 2 or 3 feet of lighter line — was spliced & hitched into the ground-line. At the end of the gangen the loop of a bowline was pushed through the eye of a fish hook, looped over & hauled taut. The ground line was made up of "shots" (50 fathom skeins) bent together. 7 shots went into one trawl tub i.e. 350 fathoms with about 670 gangens & hooks. A normal trawl might be 4 tubs — that is 1,400 fathoms (1½ miles) with 2,700 hooks! Nine dories out would put 24,000 baited hooks on the sea bottom.

Getting out the Dories Baiting was done the night before using squid or pieces of herring or mackerel. The vessel would anchor, dory hooks from the fore & main spreaders were hooked to the rope beckets at the dory bow & stern, & the dory lifted from its nest into the sea alongside, amidships. The gear was put in the dory & the crew rowed or sailed off as directed by the Captain.

The trawl sets would be as wheel spokes with the schooner as the hub.

A flying set was made when the dories were lowered & towed in 2 lines astern while the schooner jogged along. Then, as directed by the Captain, the dories would be cast off, one by one, at half-mile intervals.

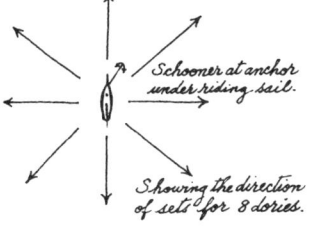
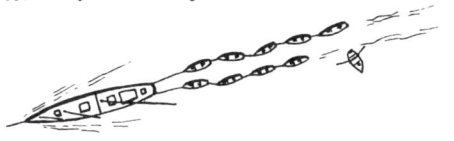

Laying the Trawl The two dorymen rowed or sailed into position. One marker buoy was dropped, the end of the ground line was bent to the anchor & the anchor let go. The bowman then paid out the trawl with its baited hooks using his "heaving stick." The sternman rowed the dory. About halfway along the trawl another marker buoy might be placed. At the end of the trawl another anchor was let go with another marker buoy. The men then waited for the fish, smoking their pipes or returning to their vessel for a "mug-up."

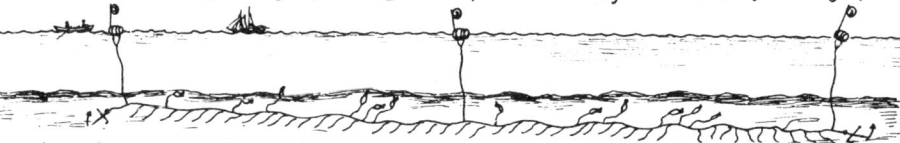

Underrunning the Trawl The trawl was hauled from one end, the ground line up one side of the dory & down the other. The bowman gaffed off the fish & the sternman rebaited the hooks as they went along the groundline. When the dory was full of fish they returned to their vessel & using two-tined pitch forks, they tossed the fish aboard.

The trawl was underun 3 or 4 times a day. A fish at every 15 hooks or so was not bad. Trawls were left in place as long as there were enough fish. The men wore woolen-knit "nippers" (gloves without thumb or fingers) while they were working the trawl. For halibut, a "gurdy" (a hand-winch) was fitted on the bow of the dory because a halibut averaged 50 pounds. A 300 pound halibut measures 6 feet from tail to snout. Lively when being hauled, halibut had to be beaten to death with a club & lashed down.

L.B. JENSON

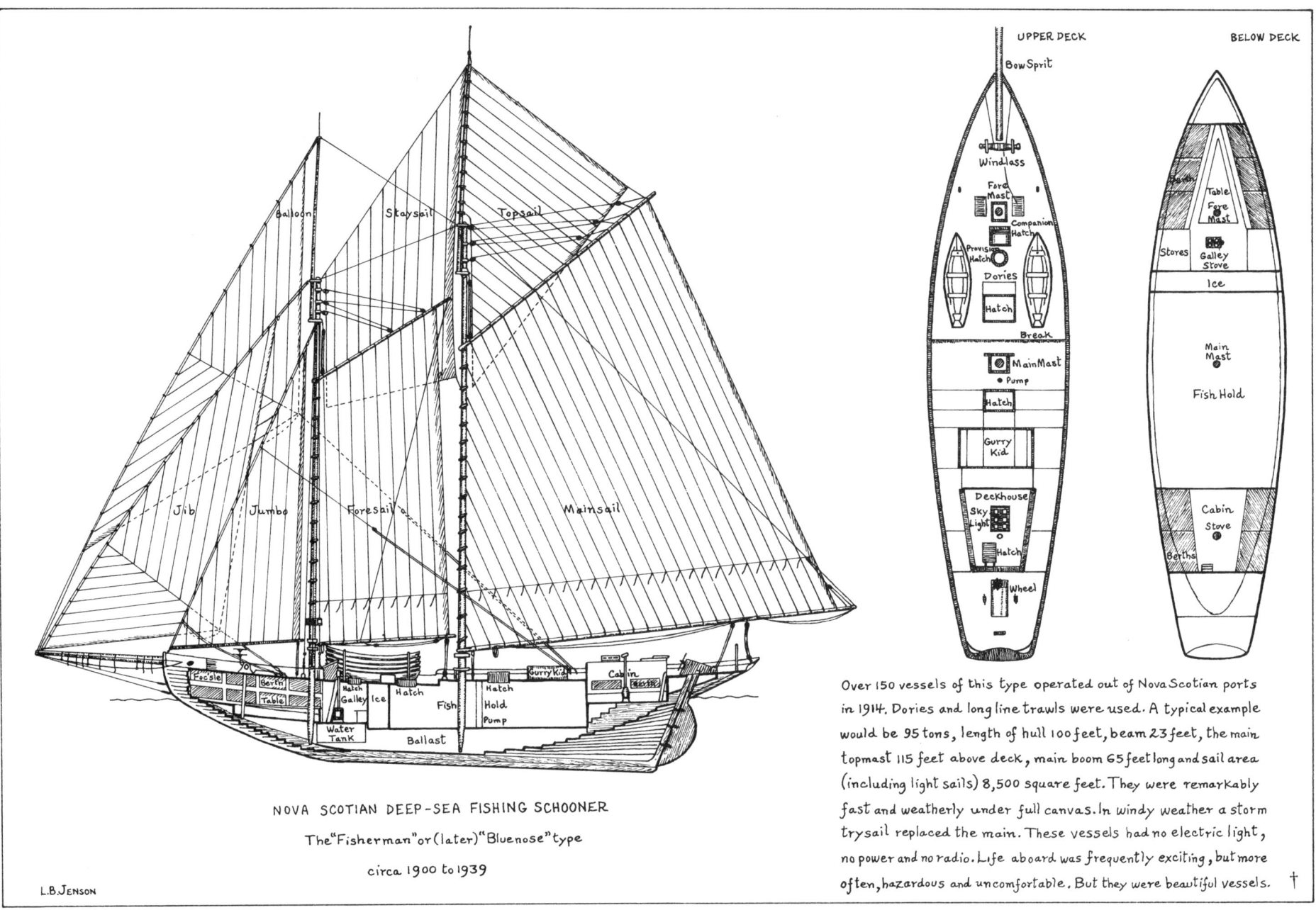

Schooner "Bluenose II"

Bluenose — Lunenburg
1921 – 1946

This sturdy little vessel is interesting because of its transom stern with the rudder fitted "outdoors." In ordinary schooners the enclosed rudder post can freeze in its trunk. With this arrangement the open rudder can be cleared of ice quite easily. Thus design is made to fit local conditions.

A Newfoundland "Jack" Schooner or Western Boat

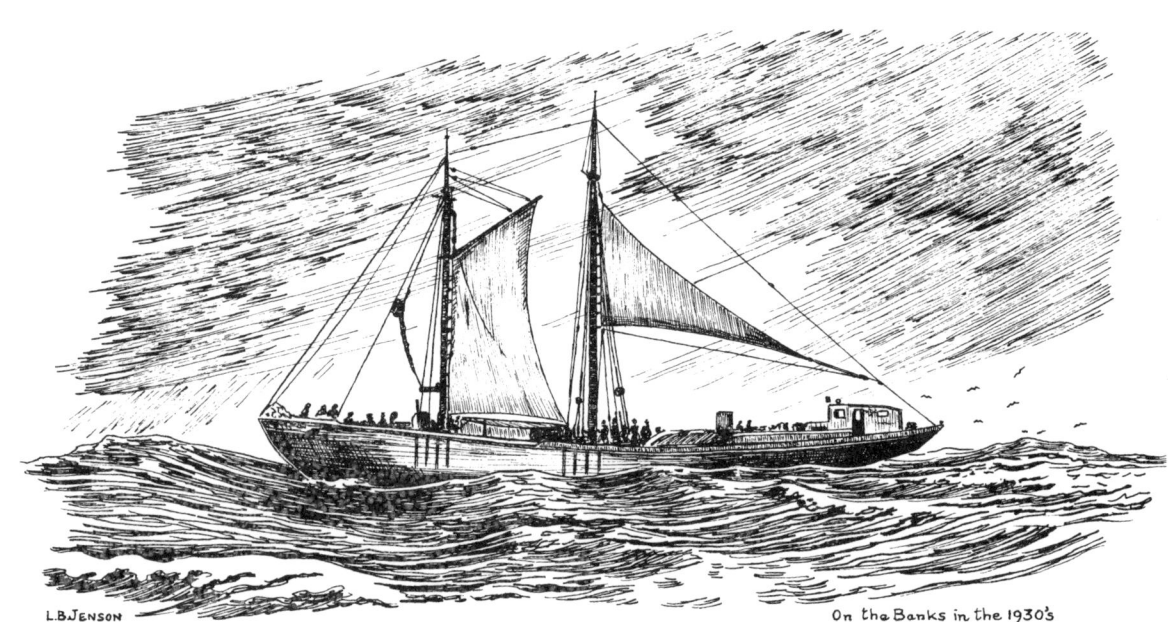

On the Banks in the 1930's

A cold, wet & hazardous occupation — this was a power schooner which fished using dories with trawls - summer & winter.

The Knockabout Schooner
— 1918 to 1949 —

In bad weather a bowsprit was a "widow maker" because so many men were lost from this spar when furling sail or working there. The bowsprit also created difficulties when manoeuvring around wharves. In 1902 Mr. McManus of Boston designed a schooner with a long overhang to replace the bowsprit. Known as "Knockabouts", they became very popular & many were built in Nova Scotia.

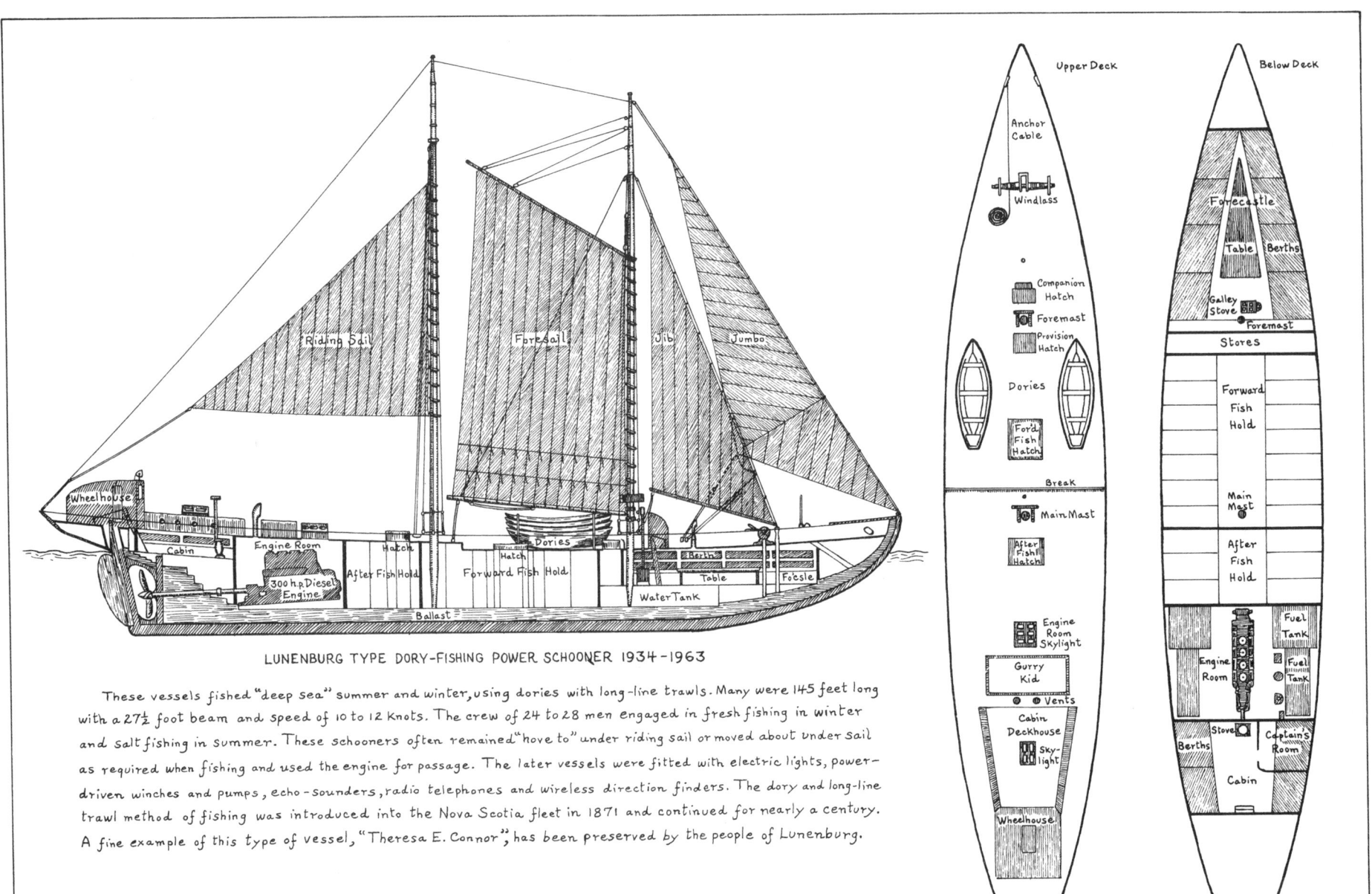

LUNENBURG TYPE DORY-FISHING POWER SCHOONER 1934-1963

These vessels fished "deep sea" summer and winter, using dories with long-line trawls. Many were 145 feet long with a 27½ foot beam and speed of 10 to 12 Knots. The crew of 24 to 28 men engaged in fresh fishing in winter and salt fishing in summer. These schooners often remained "hove to" under riding sail or moved about under sail as required when fishing and used the engine for passage. The later vessels were fitted with electric lights, power-driven winches and pumps, echo-sounders, radio telephones and wireless direction finders. The dory and long-line trawl method of fishing was introduced into the Nova Scotia fleet in 1871 and continued for nearly a century. A fine example of this type of vessel, "Theresa E. Connor", has been preserved by the people of Lunenburg.

L.B. JENSON

The Theresa E. Connor — Lunenburg

FISHERIES MUSEUM OF THE ATLANTIC
— LUNENBURG —

"Theresa E. Connor" Last of the Salt Bank Schooners

Built 1938 Length 139 feet Beam 27 feet

In 1963 "Theresa E. Connor" sailed to Newfoundland to pick up a crew for the spring trip to the Banks, but the trawlers and longliners had attracted the hands who would have been available in past years to man her dories. She slipped back to Lunenburg to lie alongside, no longer of use in the fishing industry.

In 1967, the Lunenburg Centennial Committee purchased the fine old vessel as the first phase of the Lunenburg Fisheries Museum. She was completely refitted & restored as Lunenburg's Centennial Project and now is just as she was in the days of the Salt Bank dory schooners. She is a living reminder of those days of wooden ships and iron men that are a part of the heritage of Nova Scotia.

Today, "Theresa E. Connor" proudly serves as Flagship of the small fleet of historic vessels comprising the most interesting Fisheries Museum of the Atlantic in Lunenburg.

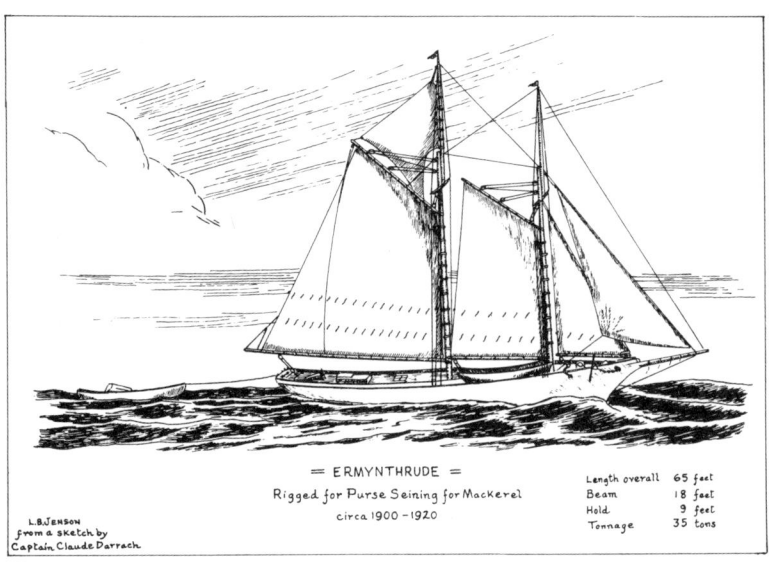

= ERMYNTHRUDE =
Rigged for Purse Seining for Mackerel
circa 1900 - 1920

Length overall 65 feet
Beam 18 feet
Hold 9 feet
Tonnage 35 tons

L.B. Jenson
from a sketch by
Captain Claude Darrach

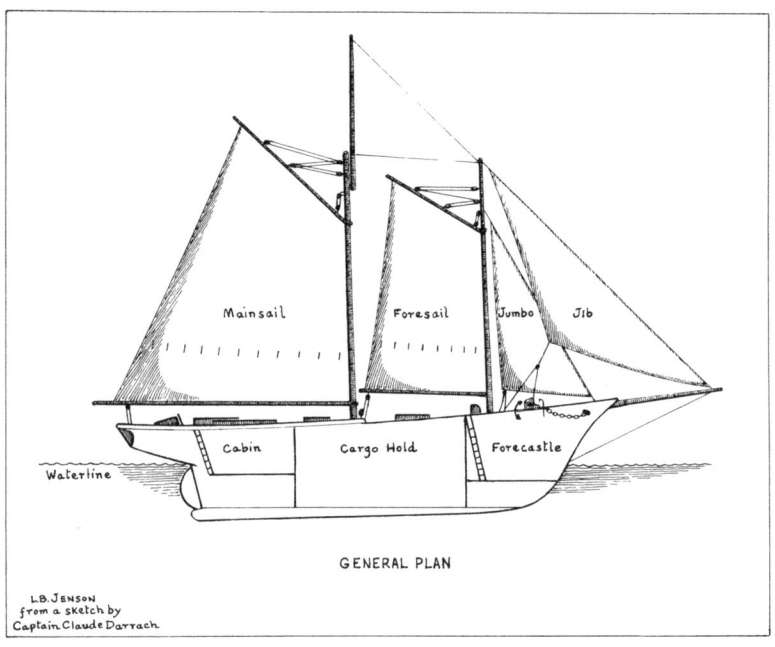

GENERAL PLAN

L.B. Jenson
from a sketch by
Captain Claude Darrach

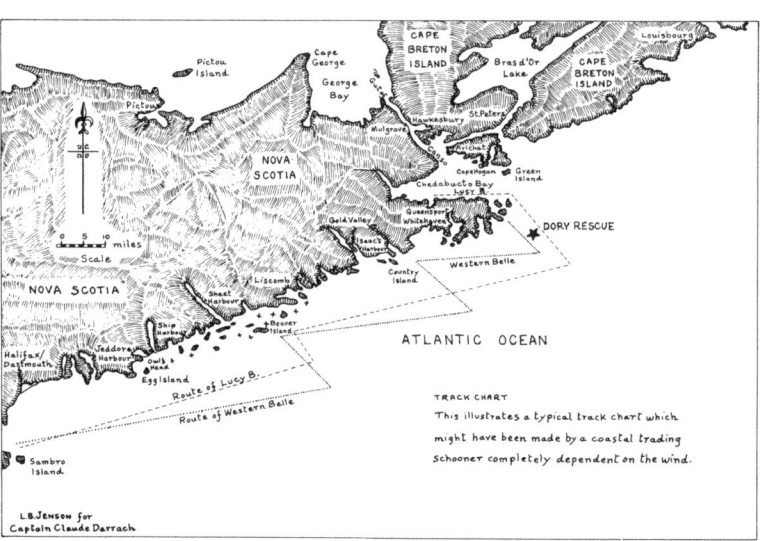

TRACK CHART
This illustrates a typical track chart which might have been made by a coastal trading schooner completely dependent on the wind.

L.B. Jenson for
Captain Claude Darrach

Coastal Schooners of Nova Scotia

These illustrations were made for "From a Coastal Schooner's Log" by Captain Claude K. Darrach published by the Nova Scotia Museum in 1979. Such schooners provided the lifeline of supplies to the outports and were the chief means of transporting their requirements and their produce for market & export. They operated until the First World War, 1914. The book is most informative, interesting and amusing.

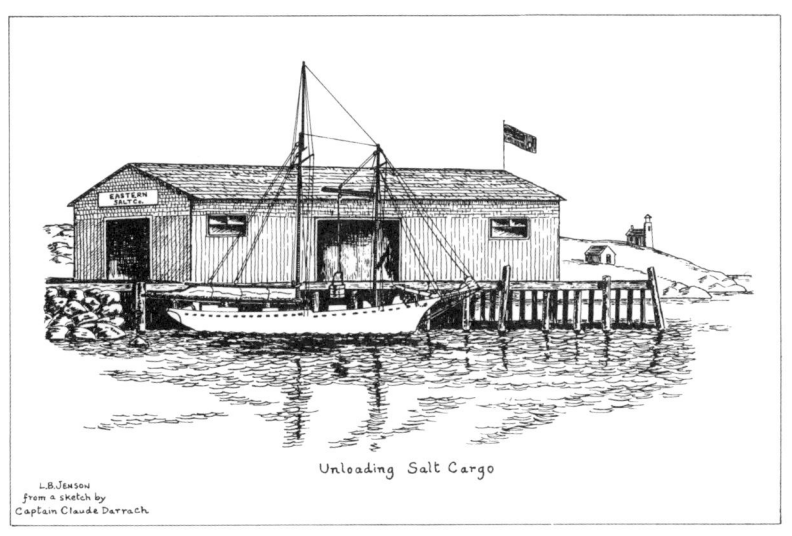

Unloading Salt Cargo

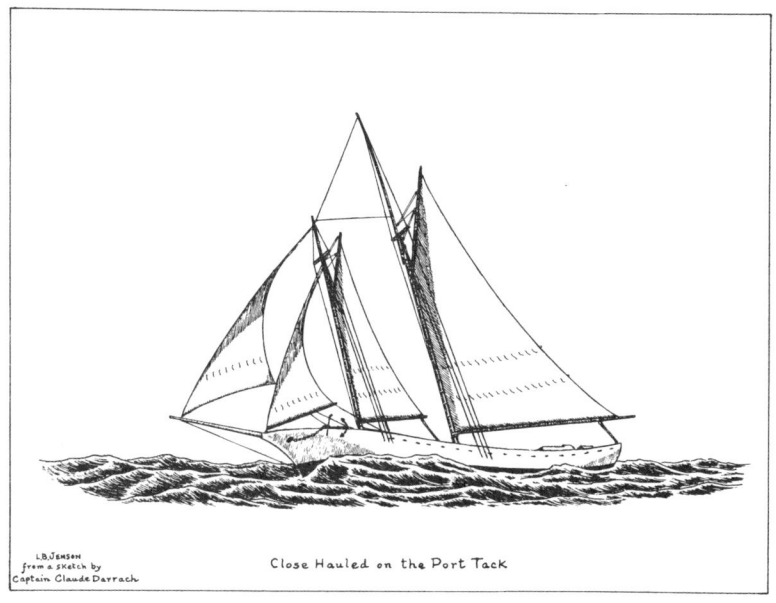

Close Hauled on the Port Tack

Reefing the Mainsail

"Containers" of an earlier age ready on a wharf,
— a typical cargo for a Schooner —

"Charles W. Morgan"
Ship-rigged Whaling Vessel, New Bedford, Massachusetts
Captain Thomas Norton
launched 21 July, 1841, by Hillman Brothers
314 gross tons, length 105.6, beam 27.7, draught 17.6

© L.B. JENSON after Captain C.M. Scammon U.S. Revenue Marine, 1874.

In 1785 a group of whalers from Nantucket settled in Dartmouth, Nova Scotia. They came for religious & commercial reasons. They were Quakers, a difficult religion in time of trouble, and since the Thirteen Colonies had become an independent country, exports to Great Britain had become subject to high tariffs. In 1791, with the encouragement of the British government, the Quaker whalers moved to Wales. One of their houses of 1785 still exists in Dartmouth. Whaling is not really a part of the Nova Scotia heritage — nevertheless, whaling was still practiced until its end in 1972.

*Whaling Ships alongside in Halifax — 1971 —

THE POTHEAD, BLACKFISH OR PILOT WHALE 20 feet

THE BLUE WHALE 98 feet

A NOTE
Canada is one of the few nations in the world with resident populations of species of whales within its national boundaries. Also, all, or most, of the great Blue Whales and the Fin Whales summer in the Gulf of St. Lawrence and present an unforgetable sight. Perhaps this page might provoke a wider interest in these wondrous creatures.

These are toothed whales. Groups of five, up to several hundreds, are not an uncommon sight. They are jet black. At one time they were killed by thousands by Newfoundlanders for mink feed. They feed mainly on squid and often enter bays. They may live for 25 years.

Blue whales are the largest animals living today. They are light blue grey in colour & live up to 100 years. They feed on krill, small shrimp-like plankton, which they strain through their black baleen. When a baleen whale gulps a mouthful of water containing food the folds allow the throat to balloon out. The whale then forces the water out & the krill etc. is strained in the frayed edges of the plates of baleen, swallowed & digested.

THE SPERM WHALE 60 feet

SOME WHALES STILL SEEN OFF NOVA SCOTIA

MEN & WHALES TO SAME SCALE

THE HUMPBACK WHALE 50 feet

The earliest true whales existed many tens of millions of years ago soon after the age of Dinosaurs. Whales include the largest animals ever to inhabit the world; they are mammals without hind legs.

TYPES OF WHALE FOOD

CAPELIN or CAPLIN

A smelt-like fish about 8 inches long, which is found in great banks. Used as cod bait.

KRILL

A small shrimp-like plankton which occurs in immense shoals. About actual size.

SQUID

A type of mollusc of varying size also found in great numbers. Used as bait & sometimes as food for humans.

These were the mainstay of the great American whaling fleets of the 18th & 19th centuries. Moby Dick was a Sperm Whale. They are brown in colour. The large teeth in the lower jaw were used for Scrimshaw. They feed mainly on large squid, usually at night and often at great depths.

Although they have been observed & hunted by man for at least three thousand years, it has become increasingly apparent that the whales are not simple creatures but are highly complex animals gifted in ways which are at present beyond our comprehension & perhaps even beyond our imagination. It is possible that whales are more intelligent than ourselves. It might well be a crime to future generations to exterminate any species of this mysterious animal.

These were declared an endangered species in 1960. They are dark above, light underneath & very "knobley." They are very acrobatic & often jump right out of the water. They feed on krill, mackerel, capelin and herring. Their spout is low & bushy, unlike other baleen whales whose spouts are high and vertical.

THE KILLER WHALE 20 feet

THE SEI WHALE 50 feet

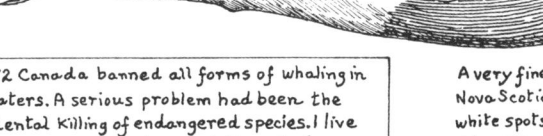

A strikingly beautiful black & white toothed whale, fairly common, hunting in small groups. They feed on cod, flatfish, herring, squid, birds, seals & young whales. They may live to 35 years. They are not dangerous to man & seem gentle & affectionate to their custodians.

In 1972 Canada banned all forms of whaling in its waters. A serious problem had been the accidental killing of endangered species. I live near an old whaling factory but I heard of no complaints when it was closed, although a good number of men lost their employment.

A very fine full sized cast of a Sei Whale may be seen in the Nova Scotia Museum. Dark above & light underneath with white spots, they feed on small plankton. Their baleen is very fine. They may live to 70 years.

L. B. JENSON

Taking a small schooner to launch — she was built in the barn to the above right
Second Peninsula, Lunenburg County

* Transporting dried codfish — Lunenburg County, 1760's to 1940's.

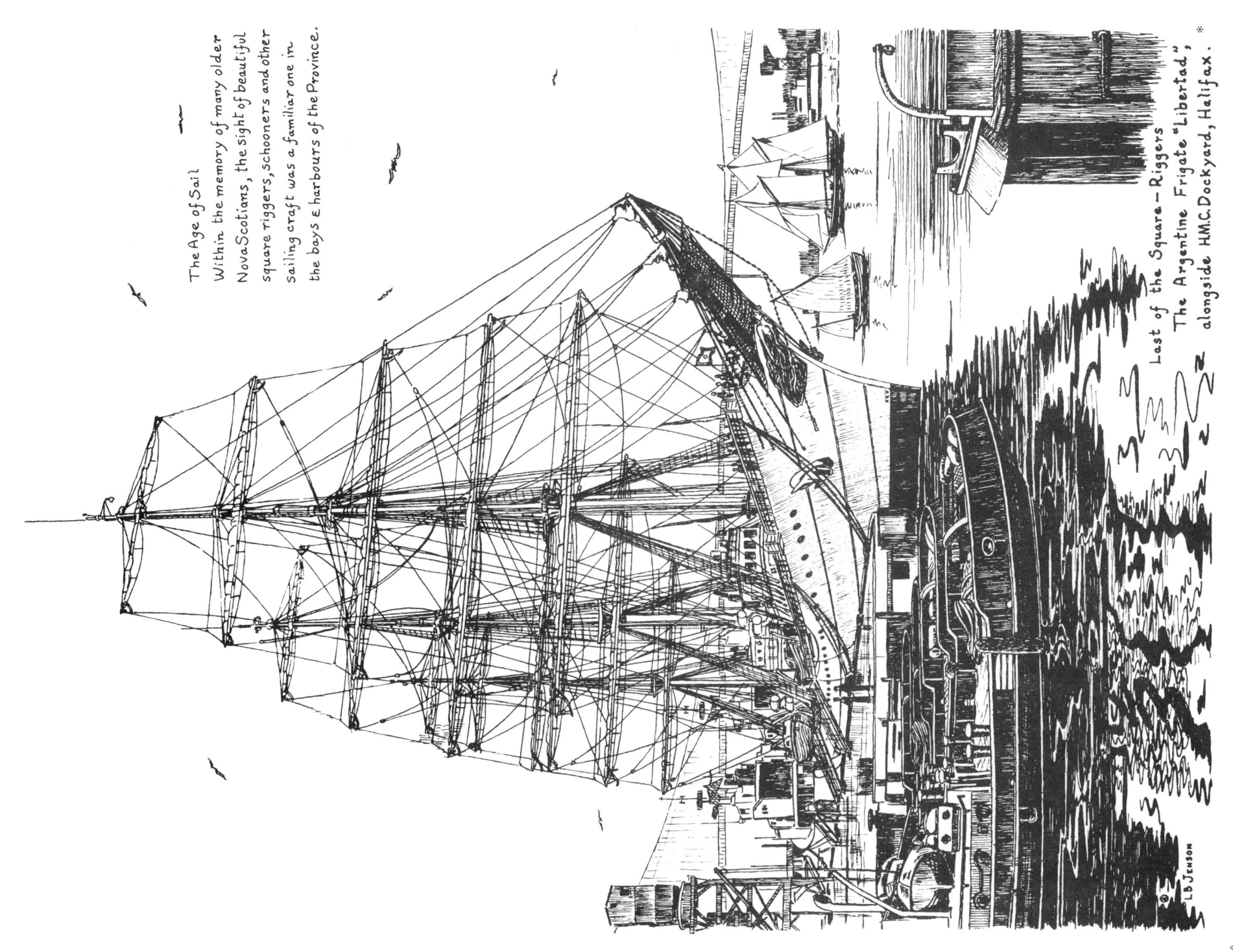

The Age of Sail
Within the memory of many older Nova Scotians, the sight of beautiful square riggers, schooners and other sailing craft was a familiar one in the bays & harbours of the Province.

Last of the Square-Riggers
The Argentine Frigate "Libertad", alongside H.M.C. Dockyard, Halifax.

1924 - The Steam Side Trawler VENOSTA - 1973

Somewhat iced-up, lying alongside in Halifax, circa 1924 to late 1940's

Vessels such as this soon proved themselves as the biggest & most reliable year-round fish catchers.

Built 1917 at Selby, England, by Cochrane & Sons Ltd., for Atlas Steam Fishing Co. of Grimsby, England. Came to Halifax, Nova Scotia, in 1924. Steam Trawlers first appeared in Canadian waters in the early 1920's. In 1926 there were 11 fishing from Nova Scotian ports.

Length 135.3 ft., Beam 23.5 feet, Draught 12.3 ft. 316 tons gross, 127 tons net. Single propeller. Triple expansion steam engine, 200 pounds pressure.

The modern development of the fresh fish processing industry regularly supplied by deep-sea trawlers has greatly enriched the economy of Nova Scotia as well as providing much employment.

L.B. Jenson
(from a photo & data kindly provided by Mr. T. Randall)

In the late 1920's & in the 1930's, the world markets for salt fish declined. Inshore fishermen & Offshore Schoonermen bitterly opposed Steam Trawlers. A Royal Commission in 1927 did not recommend further Steam Trawler development. From 1930, licenses were refused & Steam Trawlers could not clear from Canadian ports. By 1944, only 3 Steam Trawlers were fishing from Nova Scotia.

The ban on Steam Trawlers set back our fishing technology, but probably the end-result was that our many coastal communities were able to survive over many lean years.

With the end of World War Two in 1945, trawling began to replace the age-old dory method of fishing. "Cape North" & "Cape LaHave", wooden trawlers, were the first built. By 1950, five were fishing. In 1962, Canada had 37 trawlers; 28 were Nova Scotian.

The advent of the trawler & cold-storage has changed the face of our fishing industry. Large processing plants completely depend on trawlers for a year-round supply of fresh & frozen fish. Such plants employ more people than do the ships which catch the fish! The smaller Inshore fishing vessels still are vital, but except for the South-West Shore, are seasonal.

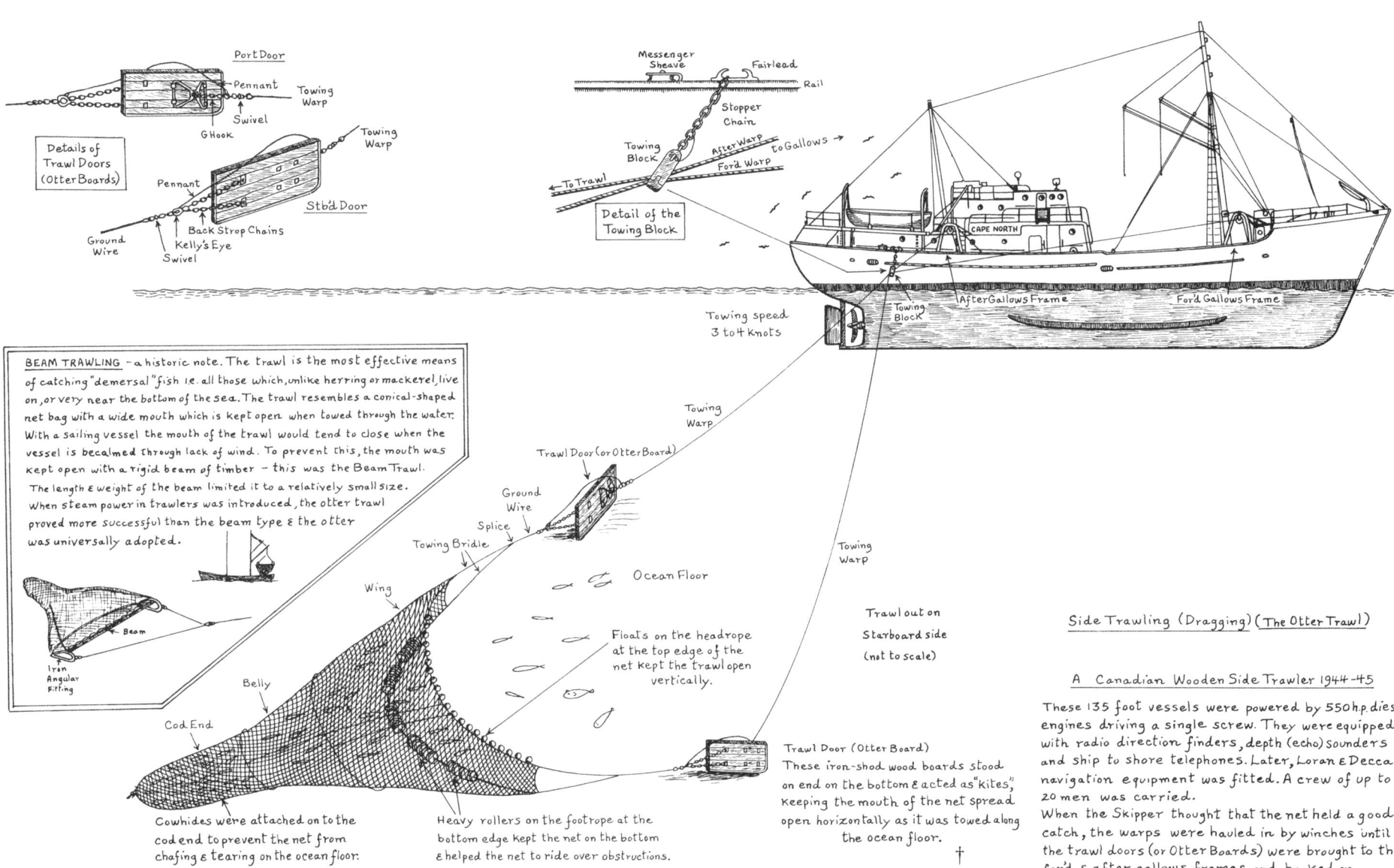

The Dragger "CAPE NORTH"

This was the first successful post World War II fresh fish trawler to be operated out of Lunenburg. She was built in Meteghan, Nova Scotia, in 1945 by Clare Shipbuilders. Her length was 135 feet and she was powered by a 550 horse power diesel engine driving a single screw. Framing & planking were of wood. Deckhouses were steel. Vessels such as this pioneered a new era in Atlantic offshore fishing.

"CAPE NORTH" now is part of the Fisheries Museum of the Atlantic at Lunenburg. She is operational in every respect from main engine to navigation aids.

L.B. JENSON

Osprey
This sea eagle is a fairly common sight over St. Margaret's Bay. It soars at 150 to 200 feet until it sights a fish. It then half-folds its wings & drops like a bolt from the blue, strikes the sea with a great splash, seizes its victim in its talons and takes off to the forest to dine at ease. It presents a spectacular sight, whether soaring, diving or flying off with a fish.

Raven
A family or clan of about a dozen Ravens lives all year-round in the forest behind my house. They take my dog's bones, share sea-food on the shore with the gulls and in season, feast on berries. They conduct noisy meetings on the ground in our cemetery & seem to enjoy gales when they soar above the breakers looking like inside-out black umbrellas.

A Raven's tail   A Crow's tail

Great Auk (Extinct)
This very large penguin used to visit St. Margaret's Bay on passage from Cape Cod to Greenland & return. It could not fly but swam rapidly on the surface. Awkward & helpless on land, the once numerous Auks were brutally clubbed to death by mariners for food, bait or sport. This cruel & thoughtless activity went on for over 300 years until they all were killed. In 1840, L. M'Kinnon & D. MacQueen in Scotland (Stac an Armin) beat one to death because they thought it was a witch.

Great Black Backed Gull
This is the largest of our Gulls and is a year-round resident of our Bay. To me this is the most attractive of all the seafowl which we can see anytime we so desire. It seems to be more reserved & dignified than the Herring Gulls.

Great Blue Heron
These beautiful & impressive birds arrive here about 6th April each year. We often see them fishing from rocks on our shore or in the marsh.

Herring Gull
Great flocks of this graceful bird are seen throughout the year on the Bay. They eat everything & anything and keep our beaches well cleared. Often one will drop a sea urchin from aloft in order to break it open.

Canada Goose
Our Bay is on the main flyway for these birds but their major stop-over is the extensive marshland around Cole Harbour on the "Eastern Shore."

Old Squaw
This diving duck is a winter resident of the Bay and is quite a common sight.

Harlequin Duck
During the winter I have seen a number of these lovely birds but they are not common.

Surf Scoter
In the fall it is quite a thrilling sight to see these birds feeding in the breaking surf. One can approach them fairly closely.

Common Loon
We seem to have Loons in the Bay most of the year except when there is much ice. Their cry always impresses me, particularly when it comes from somewhere out of a dense fog.

Black Duck
These dark brown ducks are quite common here throughout the year.

A Great Auk swimming (from an old map)

On 4th June, 1844, at Eldey in Iceland, S. Islefsson killed one male & J. Brandsson killed the female. K. Ketilson found the egg and smashed it.
This was the end.

SOME SEA BIRDS OF ST. MARGARET'S BAY, NOVA SCOTIA

L.B. JENSON

The By-gone Era of the Rum Runners —

Lying-to off the American Coast, lolling in the glassy swell, the crew sheltered under an awning, a pair of trousers drying on the davit jackstay, REO II waits to move in to the American Coast under cover of darkness or fog, without running lights, to unload her cargo of rum to the waiting speed boats of American gangsters, hard-faced, cold-eyed men — a contrast to the respected Lunenburg adventurers.

In 1920 the Americans passed the Eighteenth Amendment to their Constitution and the profitable & ancient trade of smuggling liquor was revived, in this case the illicit running to the United States of liquor of all kinds. The "drought" lasted until December 1933 when Prohibition was repealed. 1930 was the height of the Trade. When the moon was full & enterprising Nova Scotians were thus denied delivering West Indian rum or Scotch Whiskey to "dry" Americans, one might have seen 40 or more Rum Runners at anchor in St. Pierre. After 1933 some Rum Runners supplied Nova Scotians. One landing place was near my house on St. Margaret's Bay. After 1939 some Rum Runners & R.C.M.P. Marine Division served in the Royal Canadian Navy together.

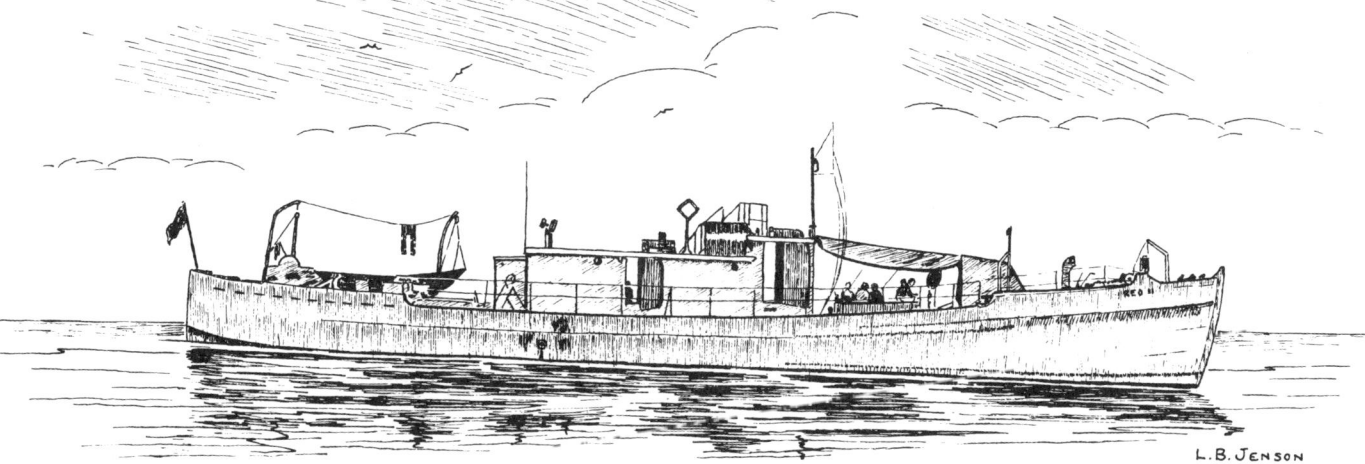

Rum Runner "REO II" about 1932

L.B. JENSON
from a photograph, courtesy Nova Scotia Museum

Built in Meteghan, Nova Scotia in 1930 specifically for the illicit trade of Rum Running, she is 104 feet long, wooden-hulled, powered by a 210 horse power diesel engine giving a speed of 10 knots. She had a low silhouette & powerful wireless radio. Her crew consisted of the Captain, Mate, 2 Engineers, Cook, Wireless Operator & 3 Deck Hands — a total of 9 men, mostly ex-fishermen. She usually operated out of Meteghan, Yarmouth & Lunenburg, running to St. Pierre Miquelon to load a cargo of spirits for "Rum Row" — the American Coast. After prohibition was repealed in the U.S.A. in 1933, she carried freight on the Eastern Shore of Nova Scotia. When war broke out in 1939, the Royal Canadian Navy commissioned her as a magnetic mine sweeper working out of Shelburne. In 1945 she became a coastal freighter in Newfoundland. The Lunenburg Fisheries Museum bought her in 1970. She is the only survivor of the Rum Running Era.

RUM !

SQUIDS & OCTOPUSES OF NOVA SCOTIA

About 40 varieties of squid & octopus (cephalopods — Greek "kephale" (head) & "podos" (foot) - the feet grow out of the head) occur in Nova Scotian waters. They are the most diverse & interesting class of molluscs. They may be thought of as wrong-side-out shellfish. Their "shell" or "pen" is compact & enclosed inside a "mantle". They have well developed heads with large eyes capable of seeing as well or better than our own.

Russian, Bulgarian & Romanian ships are among the bigger buyers of our squid for processing & freezing. Japan, China, Taiwan & Korea are a growing market for dried squid.

Drying squid is easy & cheap. No salt or preservatives are used. They are simply gutted and spread on small flakes (platforms of poles and boughs) for four or five days in dry weather. The return is $1.00 (1978) per pound.

Atlantic Long-Finned Squid.
Length 30 to 60 cm (1 to 2 feet) overall. Used for fish-bait in New England.

Eating Habits
All these creatures are carnivorous, grasping their prey with their arms or tentacles, then biting off pieces with their beak-like jaws. Squid have eight muscular arms equipped with suction cups. They also have two tentacles which are first used to seize their prey. The arms are a developement of the ordinary shellfish foot. Squid congregate in great schools.

Predators
Large fish, whales and seals eat squid and men catch them by jigging or by net.

The annual world harvest of squid is about 2 million tons.

Squid are jet-propelled. They draw water into their mantles & shoot it out backwards or forwards through a tunnel beneath the body and attain remarkable speeds.

When approached by a predator, a squid can change to a dark or another colour. They glow in the dark. To hide, they can emit a cloud of dark ink & then shoot away through the cloud, confusing the predator.

Common Squid
Length 30 cm (12 to 18 inches) overall. Fished commercially for fish bait in Nova Scotia.

Cooking a Squid (the Greeks & Romans considered cephalopods to be the finest of seafood).

Mantle — Beak — Arms & tentacles

Cut through arms & tentacles near the eyes. Squeeze out the inedible beak which will be near the cut.

Feel inside the mantle for chitinous pen & the attached visceral, pull from mantle. Wash mantle.

Cut mantle into rings, stuffing it as desired beforehand. Also the mantle can be cut as shown.

The tentacles and arms can be chopped, minced or left whole. Squid can be fried, baked etc. as desired.

Squid is an excellent source of protein, calcium, iron & phosphorus.

University News – Dalhousie 28 Oct. 77.

The Giant Squid
This great creature grows to 18 m. (50 feet) and lives in deeper waters. This "Kraken" or SeaMonster has never been proven dangerous to man!

Gourmets' Delight
Octopuses are considered good eating, at least in some parts of the world. When I tried this dish in Italy I was reminded of fried rubber bands, but my friends enjoyed their repast of sliced tentacles.

Small Octopus
It lives on the bottom in deep water.

Paper Nautilus
These live on the bottom in shallow water. Their main diet is crabs. They can change colour rapidly but usually are brown, yellow or dull rose.

L.B. JENSON
from Nova Scotia Museum and other sources.

Lower Water Street, Halifax,

A Fish Plant in Halifax — demolished 1974

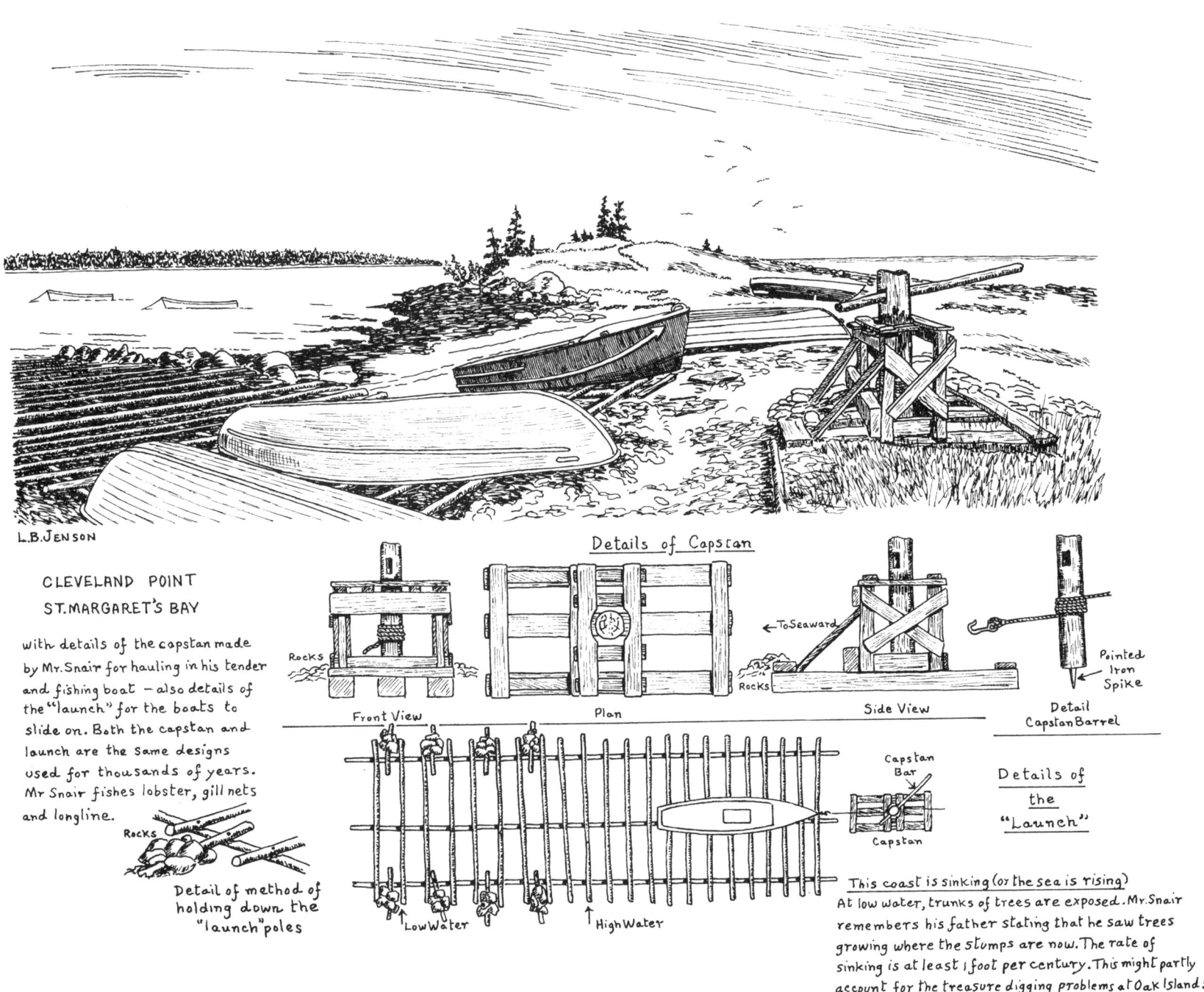

A TYPICAL NOVA SCOTIAN FISH STORE

The fish are hoisted from the boat to the wharf in tubs and taken to the cleaning table where they are cleaned, washed and then salted and stored in the large puncheons.

In these stores are the nets, floats, oars, ropes, tar, paint, the salt bin and all the odds & ends necessary to the fishermen.

The floor boards in the store are loose so that in the event of a very high tide or a storm, the seas will just lift the boards and not damage the structure of the store.

The "launch" beside the wharf is used for hauling the boats up for painting and repair or for laying up for the winter.

Most fish stores have no stove.

The rail on the wharf is for drying nets etc.

Until recently (1950), "flakes" (platforms made of boughs) were built in the nearby field. After the fish were well-soaked in salt brine, they were laid out on the flakes to dry in the sun. This preserved them for long periods, without refrigeration, even in the tropics.

Nowadays, the "pickled" fish are bought "green" & picked up by truck for commercial plants. Here they are skinned, fins cut off & then they are dried in specially heated rooms for marketing.

L.B. JENSON

L.B. Jenson

Old Lower Water Street, Halifax — 1979.

The two buildings on the left house the Federal Department of Fisheries Research Laboratory, in the centre is the Robertson Building being altered to be the offices of the Maritime Museum of the Atlantic & on the right, the main Post Office (until 1979).

The Fisheries Research Laboratory was established in 1924. The development of the fresh fish processing industry has added much wealth & employment to Nova Scotia & this laboratory has contributed a great deal to this development. In cooperation with the Nova Scotia Department of Fisheries it has been in the forefront of all the modern sophistication & technological advances, not only in fish processing, but in fishing techniques, design of fishing vessels, development of new gear, usage of new nets, containers, transhipment, storage and even new fish dishes. They have made demonstration facilities available both to fishermen & processors. The Laboratory introduced the power block here and revolutionized our herring fishery. They have scouted around the world to be aware & up to date on all the new fish-catching methods & have demonstrated them to local fishermen. They have been the single counterpart in Nova Scotia to the agricultural research stations. The total staff is 79 & is made up of 18 PhD's, 16 chemists, 6 engineers, 2 bacterialologists, 1 home economist with the remainder being technicians of various types.

Despite our great experience in fishing, our real knowledge of fish & their ways remains very limited indeed.

Fishing must be of ever-increasing importance to Canada & the world. Continuing research is vital to us all.

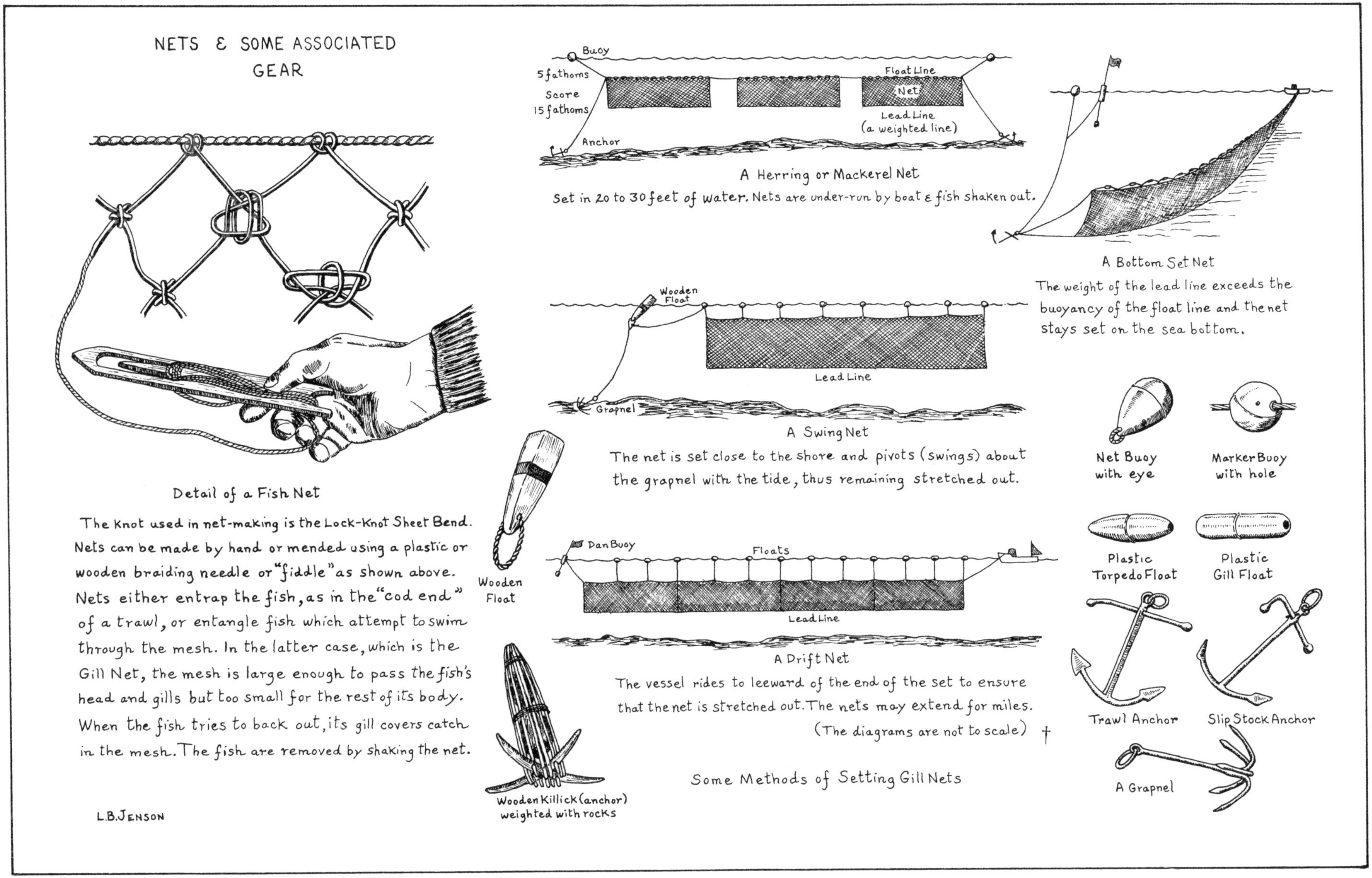

NETS & SOME ASSOCIATED GEAR
Detail of a Fish Net
The knot used in net-making is the Lock-Knot Sheet Bend. Nets can be made by hand or mended using a plastic or wooden braiding needle or "fiddle" as shown above. Nets either entrap the fish, as in the "cod end" of a trawl, or entangle fish which attempt to swim through the mesh. In the latter case, which is the Gill Net, the mesh is large enough to pass the fish's head and gills but too small for the rest of its body. When the fish tries to back out, its gill covers catch in the mesh. The fish are removed by shaking the net.
L.B.JENSON
Buoy
5 fathoms
Score
15 fathoms
Anchor
Float Line
Net
Lead Line
(a weighted line)
A Herring or Mackerel Net
Set in 20 to 30 feet of water. Nets are under-run by boat & fish shaken out.
A Bottom Set Net
The weight of the lead line exceeds the buoyancy of the float line and the net stays set on the sea bottom.
Wooden Float
Lead Line
Grapnel
A Swing Net
The net is set close to the shore and pivots (swings) about the grapnel with the tide, thus remaining stretched out.
Net Buoy with eye
Marker Buoy with hole
Plastic Torpedo Float
Plastic Gill Float
Wooden Float
Dan Buoy
Floats
Lead Line
A Drift Net
The vessel rides to leeward of the end of the set to ensure that the net is stretched out. The nets may extend for miles.
(The diagrams are not to scale) †
Trawl Anchor
Slip Stock Anchor
A Grapnel
Wooden Killick (anchor) weighted with rocks
Some Methods of Setting Gill Nets

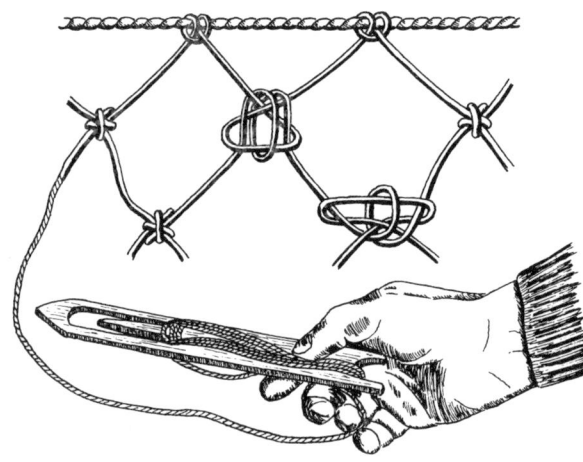

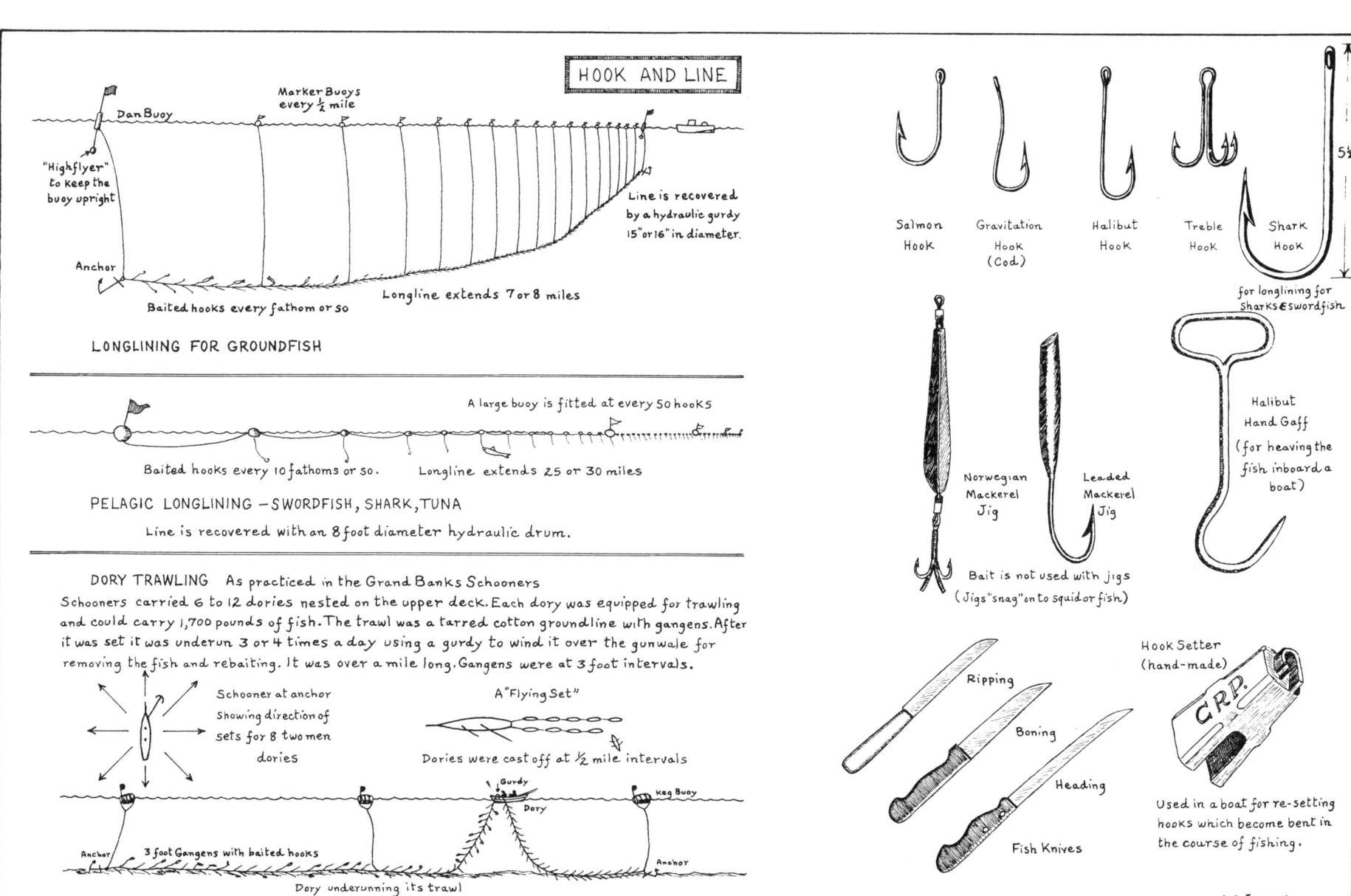

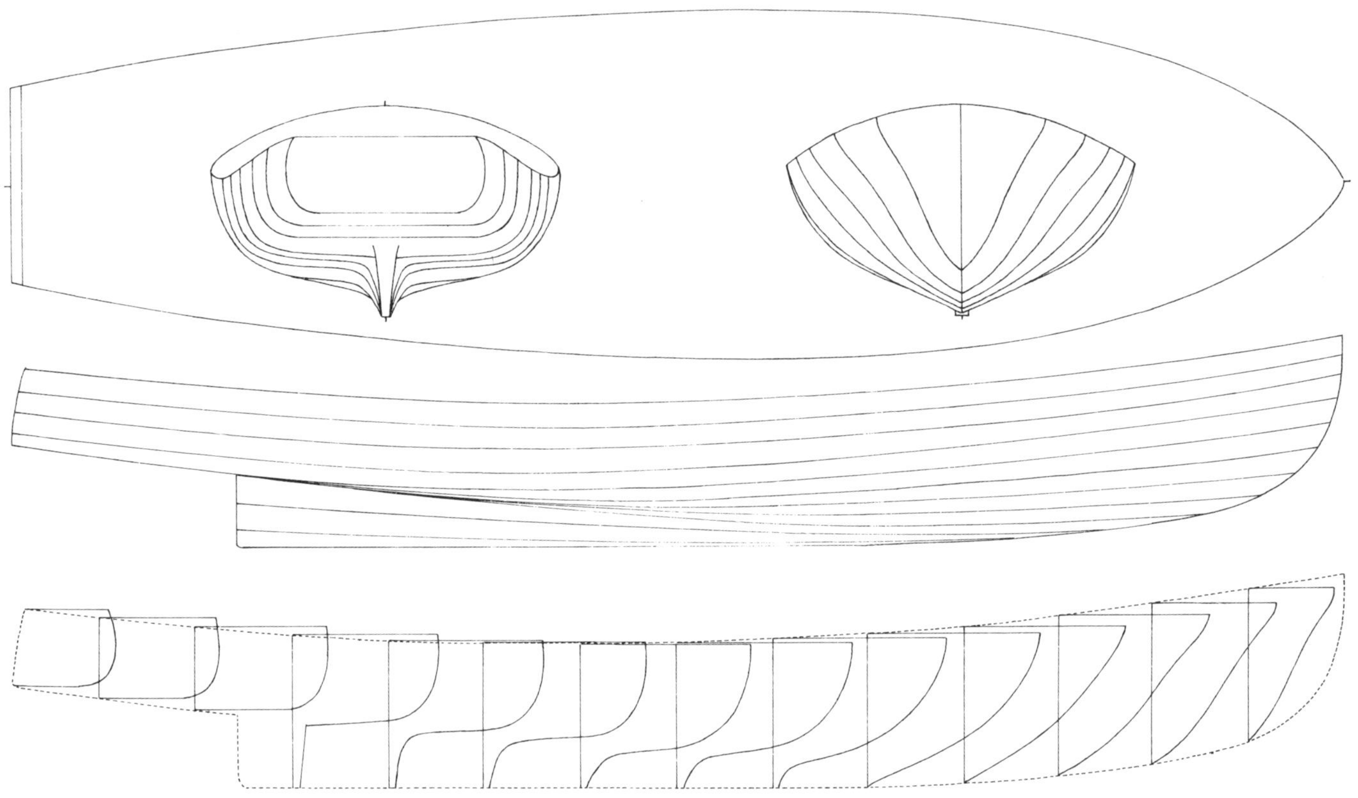

L.B.JENSON

Half Hull for a Cape Islander
carved by Mr. W.J.Roué, designer of
the original Bluenose

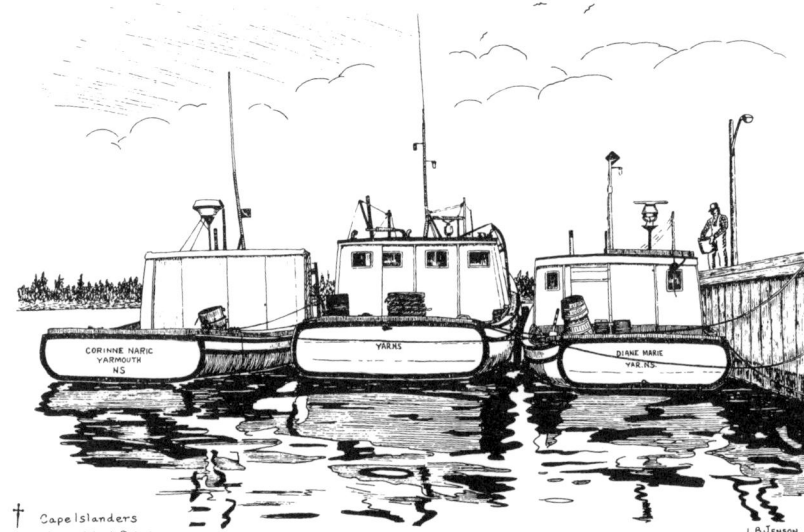

† Cape Islanders
Lower West Pubnico

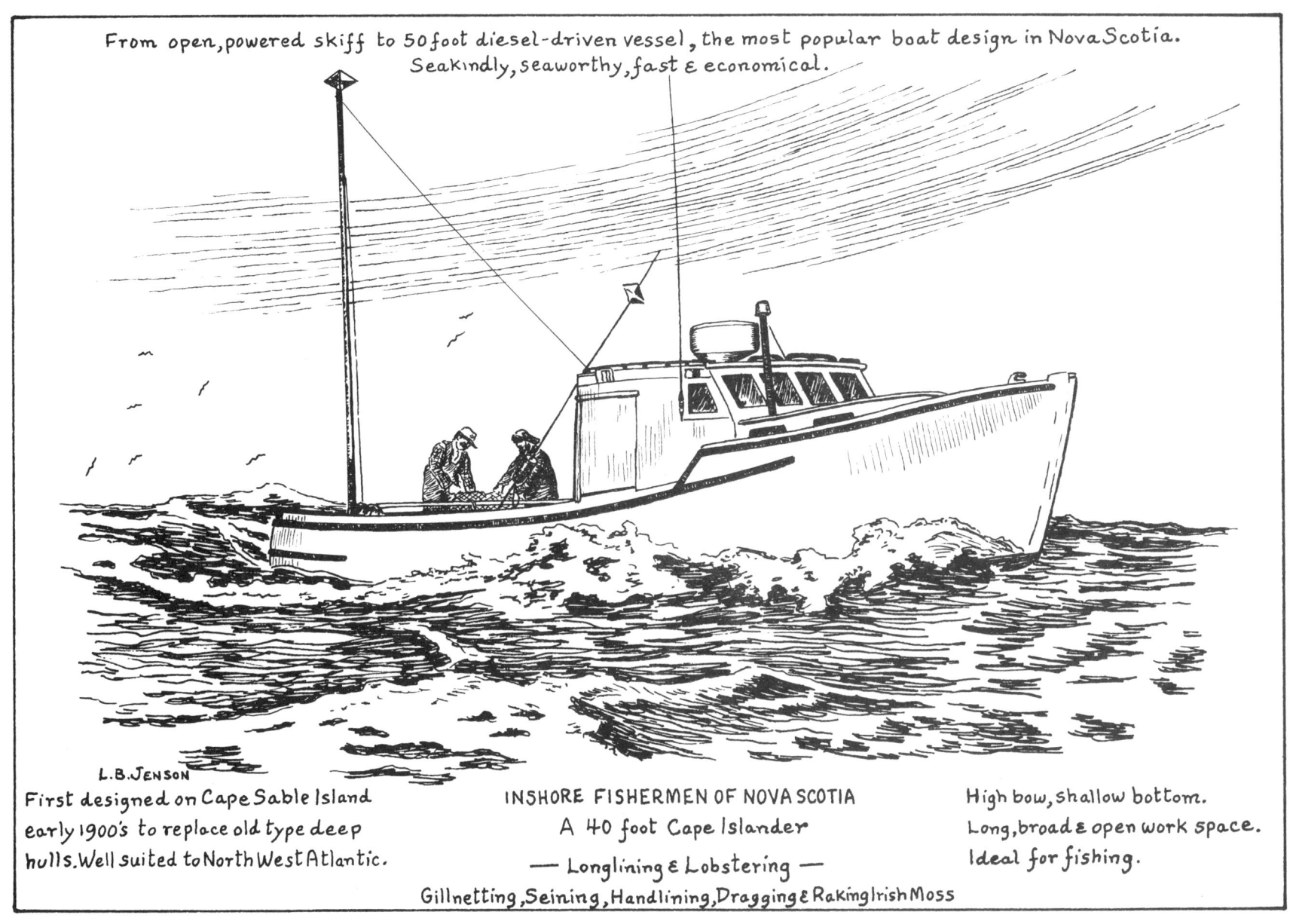

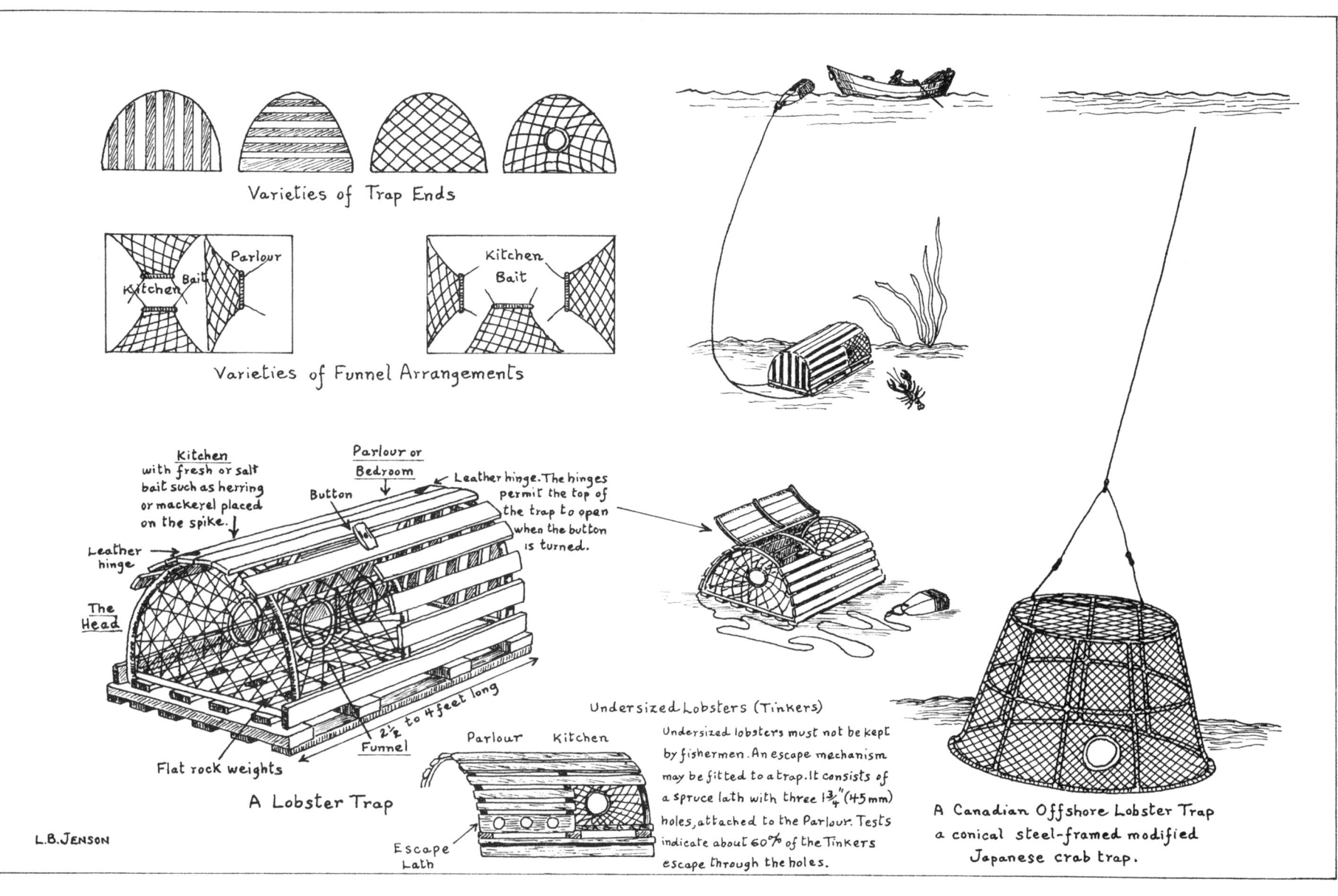

Making Lobster Traps Lunenburg County

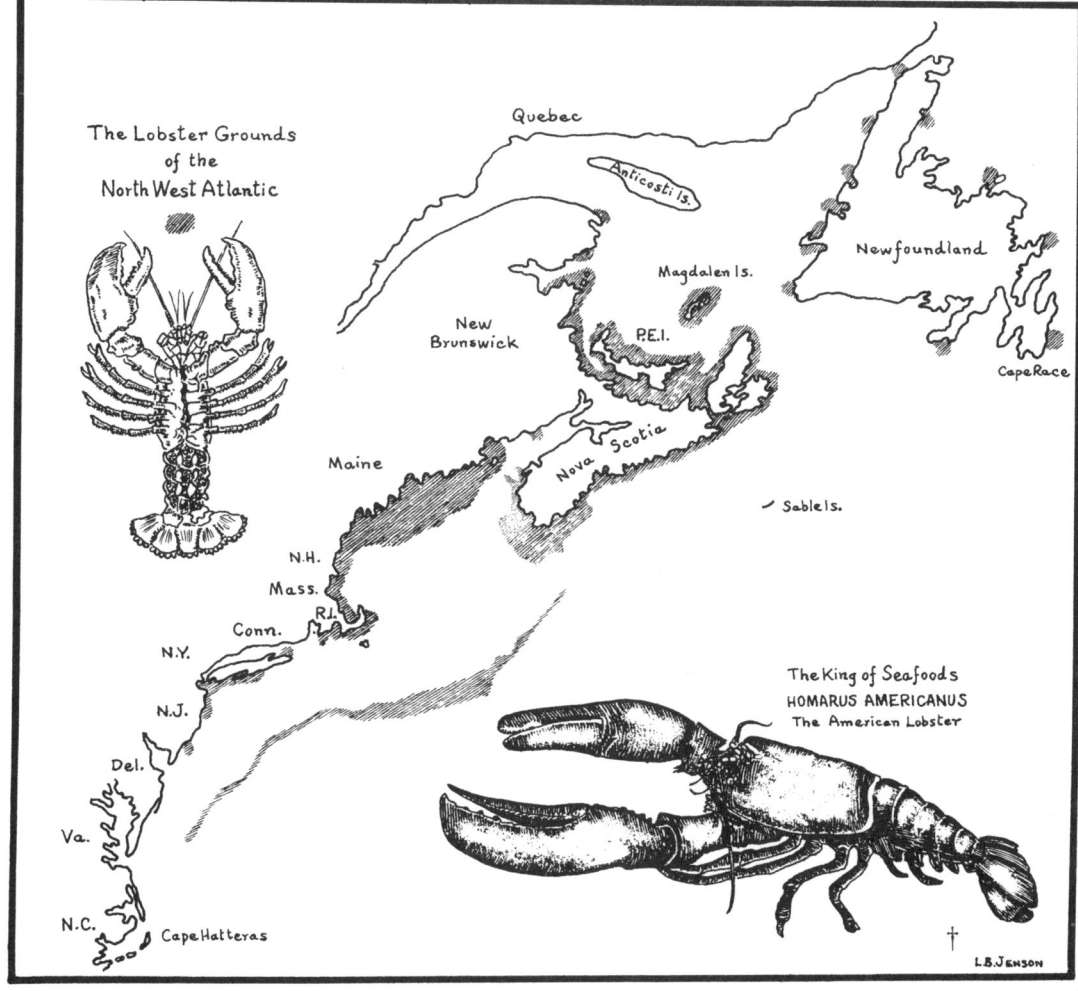

The Lobster Grounds of the North West Atlantic

The King of Seafoods
HOMARUS AMERICANUS
The American Lobster

The Lobster Fishing Season—
Inshore Fishermen headed out to sea to lay their traps on the opening day of the season.

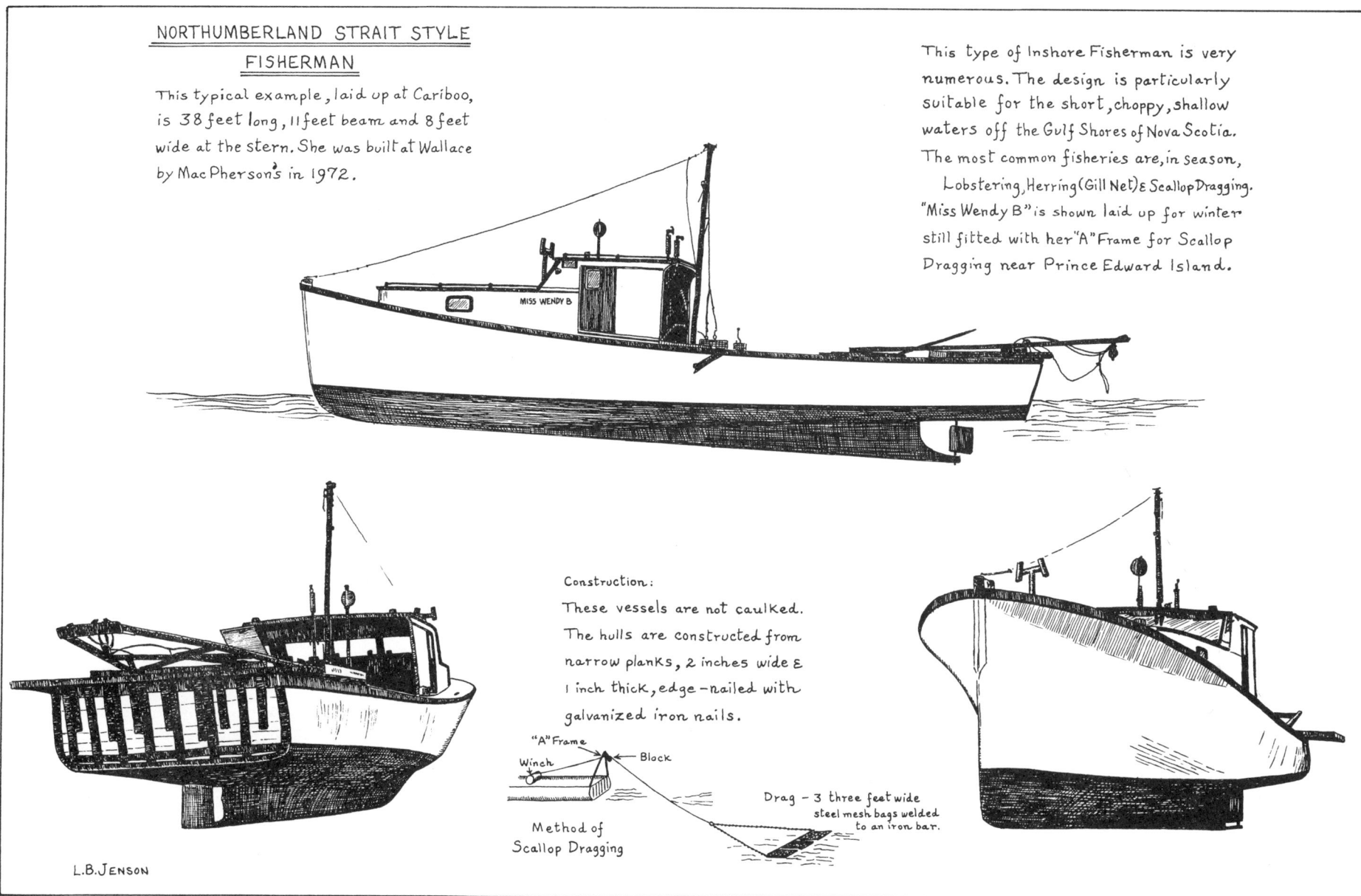

NORTHUMBERLAND STRAIT STYLE FISHERMAN

This typical example, laid up at Cariboo, is 38 feet long, 11 feet beam and 8 feet wide at the stern. She was built at Wallace by MacPherson's in 1972.

This type of Inshore Fisherman is very numerous. The design is particularly suitable for the short, choppy, shallow waters off the Gulf Shores of Nova Scotia. The most common fisheries are, in season, Lobstering, Herring (Gill Net) & Scallop Dragging. "Miss Wendy B" is shown laid up for winter still fitted with her "A" Frame for Scallop Dragging near Prince Edward Island.

Construction:
These vessels are not caulked. The hulls are constructed from narrow planks, 2 inches wide & 1 inch thick, edge-nailed with galvanized iron nails.

Method of Scallop Dragging

Drag - 3 three feet wide steel mesh bags welded to an iron bar.

L.B. JENSON

Mr. R. Baker preparing his long-liner for the inshore fishery, —Greater Tancook Island

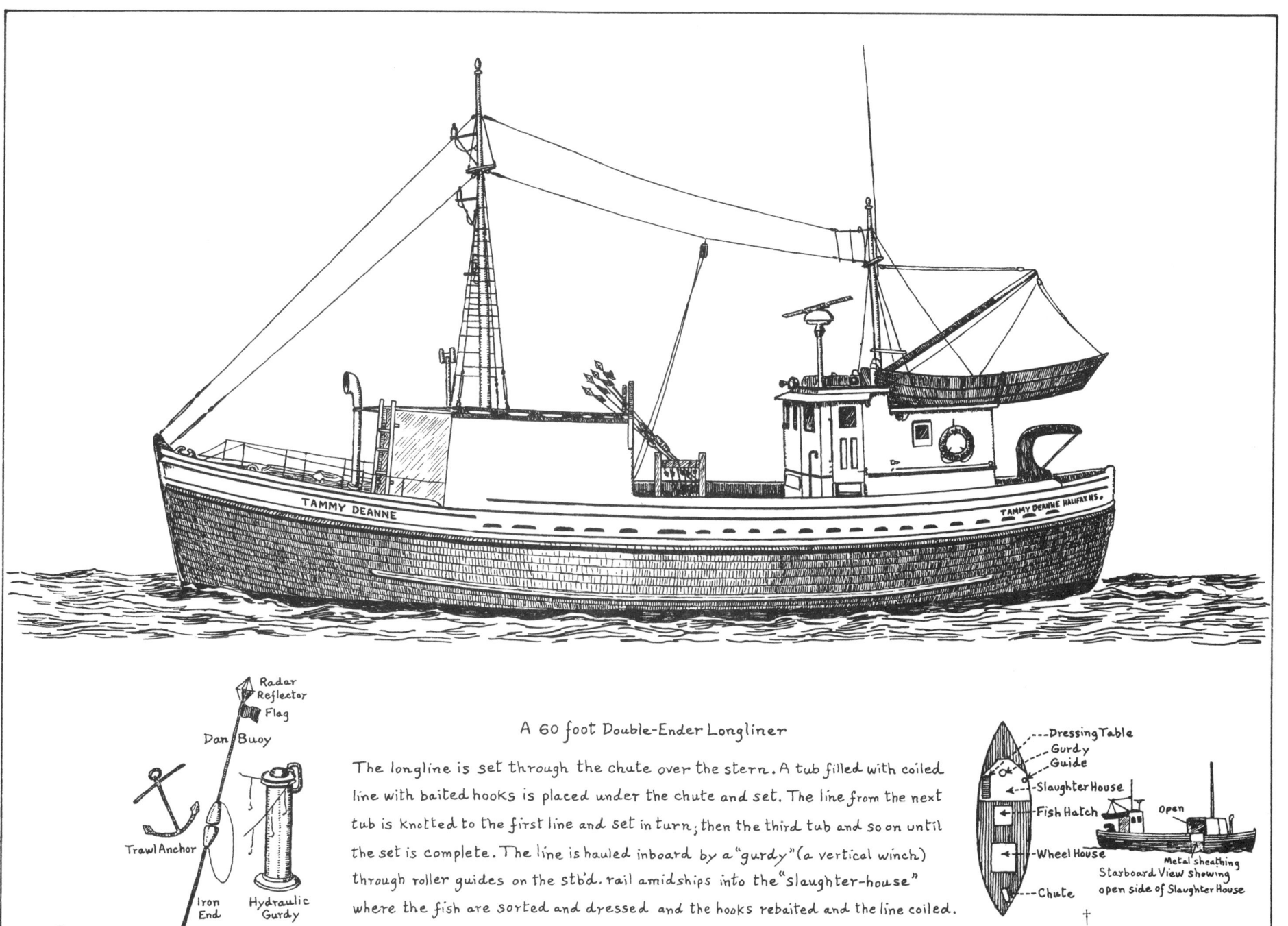

A 60 foot Double-Ender Longliner

The longline is set through the chute over the stern. A tub filled with coiled line with baited hooks is placed under the chute and set. The line from the next tub is knotted to the first line and set in turn; then the third tub and so on until the set is complete. The line is hauled inboard by a "gurdy" (a vertical winch) through roller guides on the stb'd. rail amidships into the "slaughter-house" where the fish are sorted and dressed and the hooks rebaited and the line coiled.

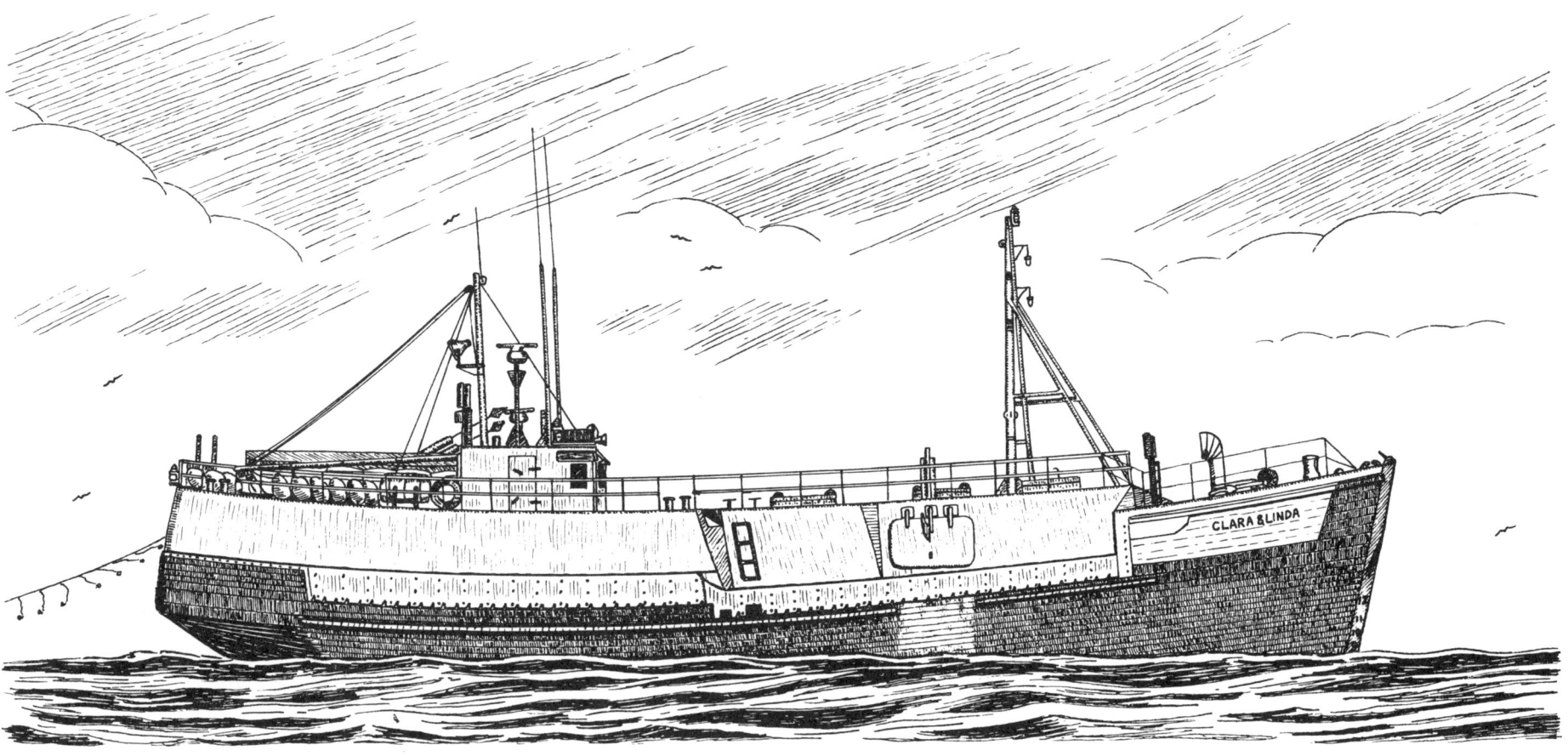

L.B. JENSON

"CLARA & LINDA"
93 foot Automated Longliner, Hubbards, Nova Scotia
— Maxcatch Fisheries, Brian Shebib, Owner. Began April, 1977. —

Crew — Captain and 6 Hands

Catch — Cod & Hake for Salt Fish trade

This vessel is unique in North America, being the first successful automated longliner in these waters. "Clara & Linda" was converted from a standard longliner by the fitting of "Mustad Autoline System" from Norway and an aluminum superstructure built over it in Hubbards. Advantages of longlining include selective fishing; only certain species & sizes of fish can take the baited hooks. The disadvantage has been the long and tedious task of baiting hooks & hand-coiling the lines down in tubs. Six earlier attempts were made to automate longlining in Canadian vessels but they failed. The system is operating in Norway, the Faeroes & Iceland. The line is baited with mackerel, cut up by machine, at up to 5 hooks a second, right at the stern & paid out through a square hatch on the port side of the stern. Up to 17,000 hooks a day have been baited. The gangions (short lines, each with 1 hook) are spaced 42 inches so that amounts to about 12 miles of line. The gear is recovered by winch through the hatch on the starboard side; the fish are removed by hand or gaff and the machine then scrubs the hooks of bait & weeds, removes twists in the gangions, separates the hooks & hangs them on a rack above the rolls of line & then feeds the gear into the bait machine again. The crew sort, clean & stow the fish in ice in the hold. "Clara & Linda" fishes on the Grand Banks, winter trips are 14 days & summer trips 12 or 10 days. This system shows great promise for Canadian Fishermen.

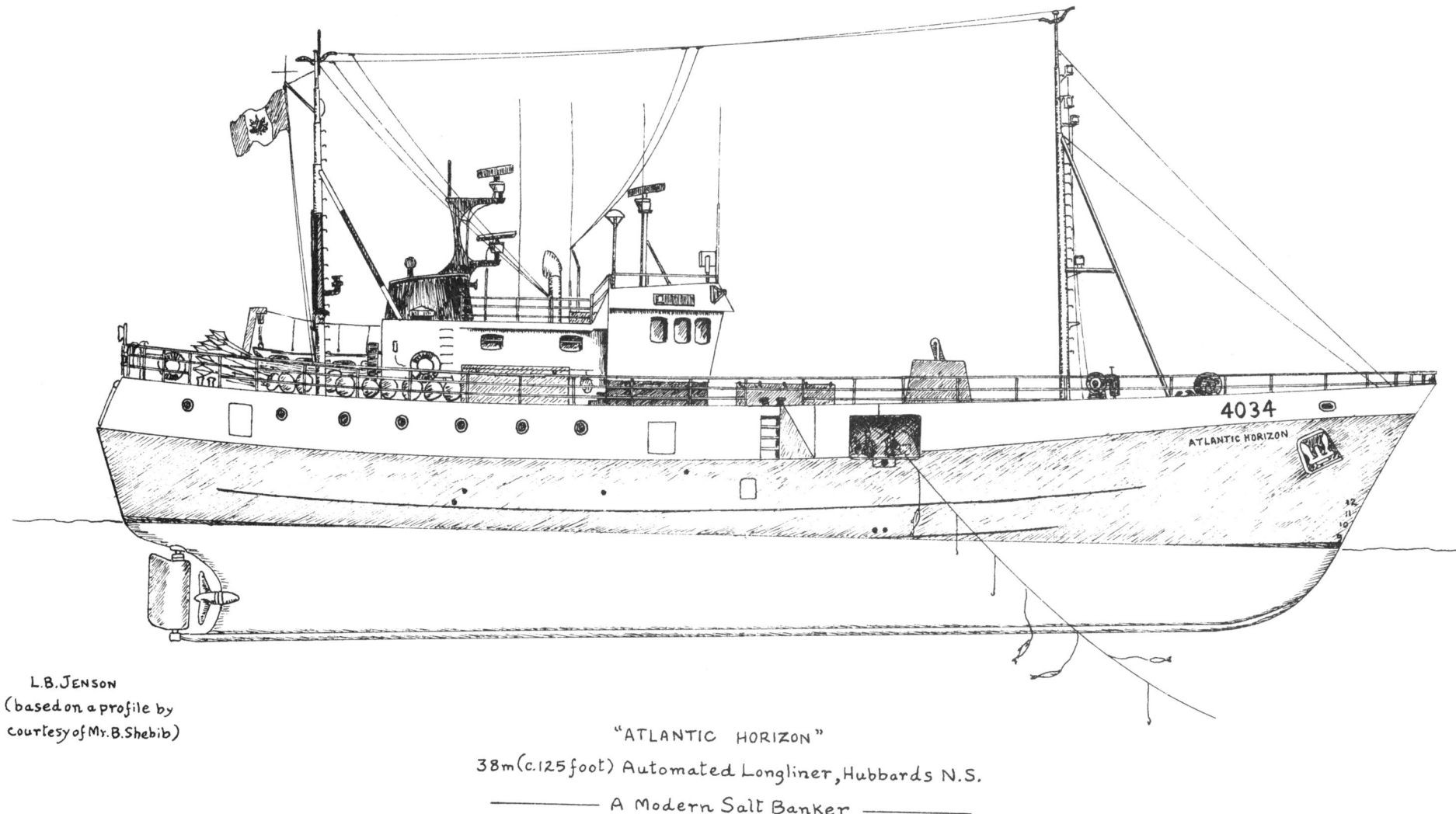

L.B. JENSON
(based on a profile by
courtesy of Mr. B. Shebib)

"ATLANTIC HORIZON"
38m (c.125 foot) Automated Longliner, Hubbards N.S.
———— A Modern Salt Banker ————

This vessel was built in Norway for the Faeroe Islands fishery. She was purchased by Maxcatch Fisheries and began fishing on the Grand Banks in 1979. She is fitted with the Mustad Autoline System similar to that fitted in "CLARA & LINDA". In addition she is fitted with a machine which "splits" the cod so that they can be salted immediately. By the time she has a full catch and returns to Hubbards the fish are well advanced in their "cure."

PURSE-SEINING

The purse-seine is a net which can be "pursed-up" to trap a school of fish. It is particularly suitable for certain migratory species. The net is stowed at the stern of the Seiner, the top with the floats on one side and the weighted bottom on the other to prevent the net from twisting when it is set, or "shot" over the stern.
When a school is located, a small skiff is launched from the Seiner and rowed off towing one end of the seine net.
The Seiner then travels in a circle to surround the school of fish and the net is paid out. Both ends finally are brought together. The purse-line around the bottom of the net then is drawn in gradually until the bottom is closed and the fish cannot escape. The ends of the net now are hauled inboard the Seiner until the fish are massed together in a small area.
A dip net or "brailer" scoops loads of fish from the seine net and drops them into the fish hold or into a packer boat to be taken to a cannery.

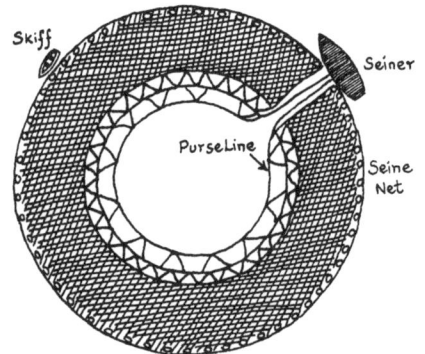

(not to scale)

A Nova Scotian Herring Seiner

A pump on the port side amidships is put into the sea to suck the fish out of the purse seine net. Fish and water are separated inboard, the water goes over the side and the fish chute down the hold. The net is hauled aboard on the starboard side by the power block at the end of the boom (which would be raised). The smaller boom is used for brailing fish from the net when so required. The power skiff is carried on top of the nets bow first on the stern and slid over the transom to set the purse seine net and push the seiner into position. A 60 foot double-ended Herring Carrier shown lying off, works with the Seiner.

L.B. JENSON

Power Skiff

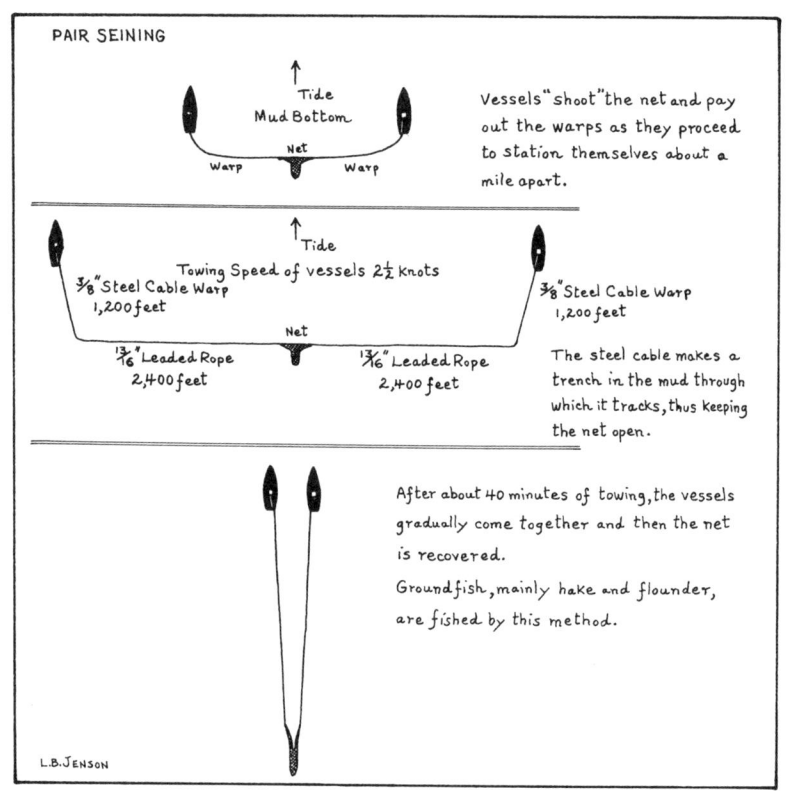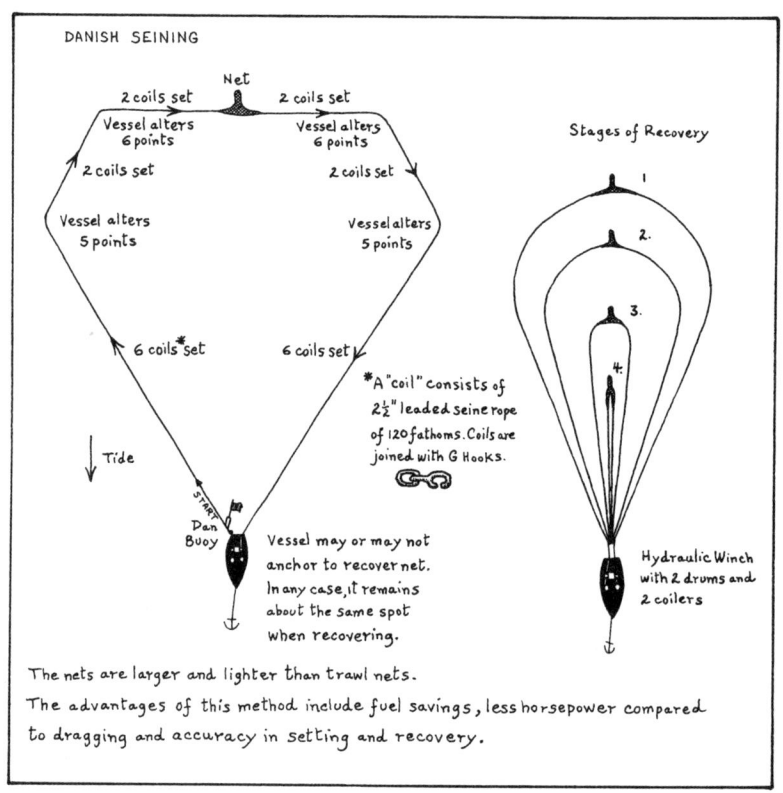

"SEALIFE II"
Pictou, Nova Scotia.
Danish/Scottish Seiner

St. Margaret's Bay Seines

These attractive lap-work (clinker) boats, built locally, are 28 feet long with an 8 foot beam and are capable of carrying up to 9,000 pounds of fish. They are used to tend the fish traps around the Bay & are considered ideal for handling nets and gear in the relatively sheltered waters of St. Margaret's.

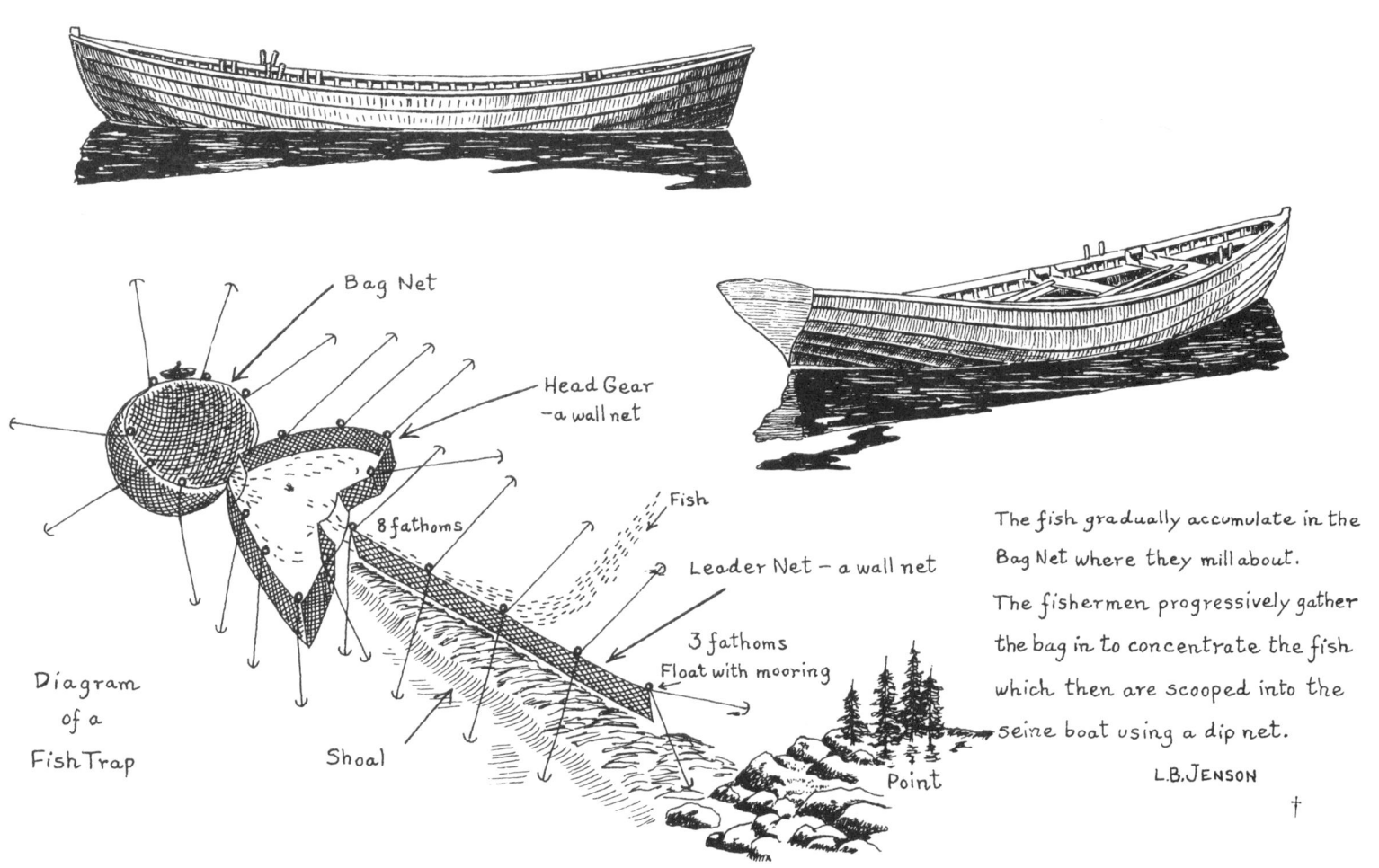

The fish gradually accumulate in the Bag Net where they mill about. The fishermen progressively gather the bag in to concentrate the fish which then are scooped into the seine boat using a dip net.

L.B. JENSON

This information was kindly provided by Mr. Robert Conrad.

St. Margaret's Bay Fishery — Tuna etc.

The motorboat is towing a fleet of "seines." A wide variety of fish is caught in net "traps". They are then transferred to a seine-boat by dip-net. The "stand" or "pulpit" on the bow was for harpooning tuna but this practice is not allowed now and the stands are not fitted anymore.

Blue fin tuna follow the smaller fish into the traps. The fishermen force the tuna into separate "pounds" where they are fed and kept until required.

Mr. Robert Conrad is in the lead boat.

L.B. Jenson

Catches

Lobster	— spring and late fall
Cod	— spring to fall
Blue fin Tuna	— mid-June to late August
Mackerel	— late spring/early summer

A Fishing Weir in the Bay of Fundy
Conflict of interest can arise between weir operators and seiners.

The Bay of Fundy —
where the tidal range is forty feet, the greatest in the world.
As the tide goes out fish are captured in weirs such as this.

NOVA SCOTIA SCALLOP DRAGGERS

Fishermen are of a sturdy, independent nature but are prepared to band together in the interest of conserving fish stocks. In this case, experience has shown that if limits are not placed on the harvest of the valuable resource of scallops, this shellfish will cease to be of commercial importance & many fishermen and plant workers will lose employment.

This also was an opportunity to show the hardy type of men who follow the hazardous life of fishing the stormy North Atlantic. The larger Scallop Draggers sailing out of Lunenburg, Riverport & Shelburne, fish on Georges Bank. The smaller Fundy vessels fish Browns Bank & the Bay of Fundy.

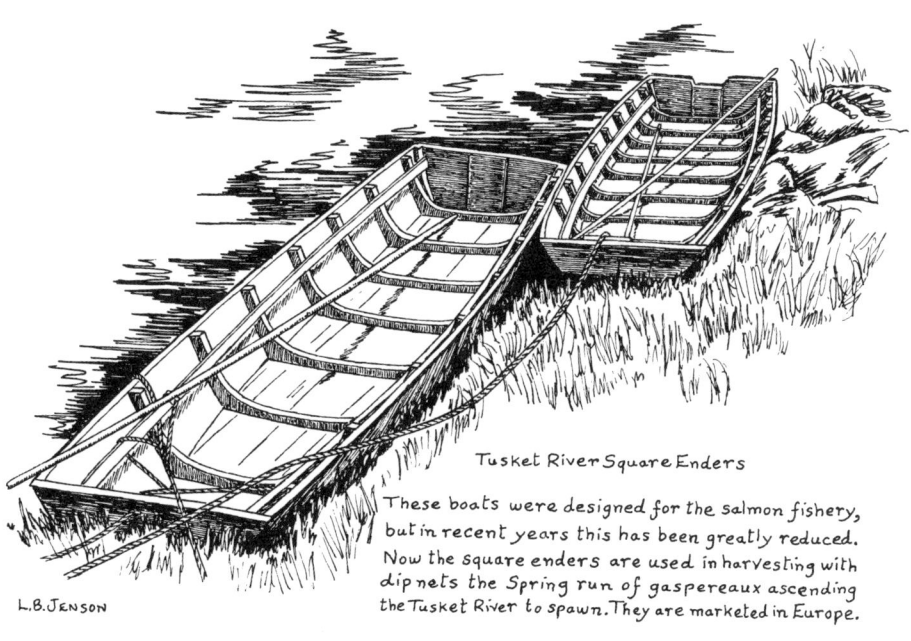

Tusket River Square Enders

These boats were designed for the salmon fishery, but in recent years this has been greatly reduced. Now the square enders are used in harvesting with dip nets the Spring run of gaspereaux ascending the Tusket River to spawn. They are marketed in Europe.

CONSERVATIONISTS

Nova Scotian Scallop Fishermen refused to sail until the Federal Government restored the 180,000 pound catch limit per quarter, per vessel.

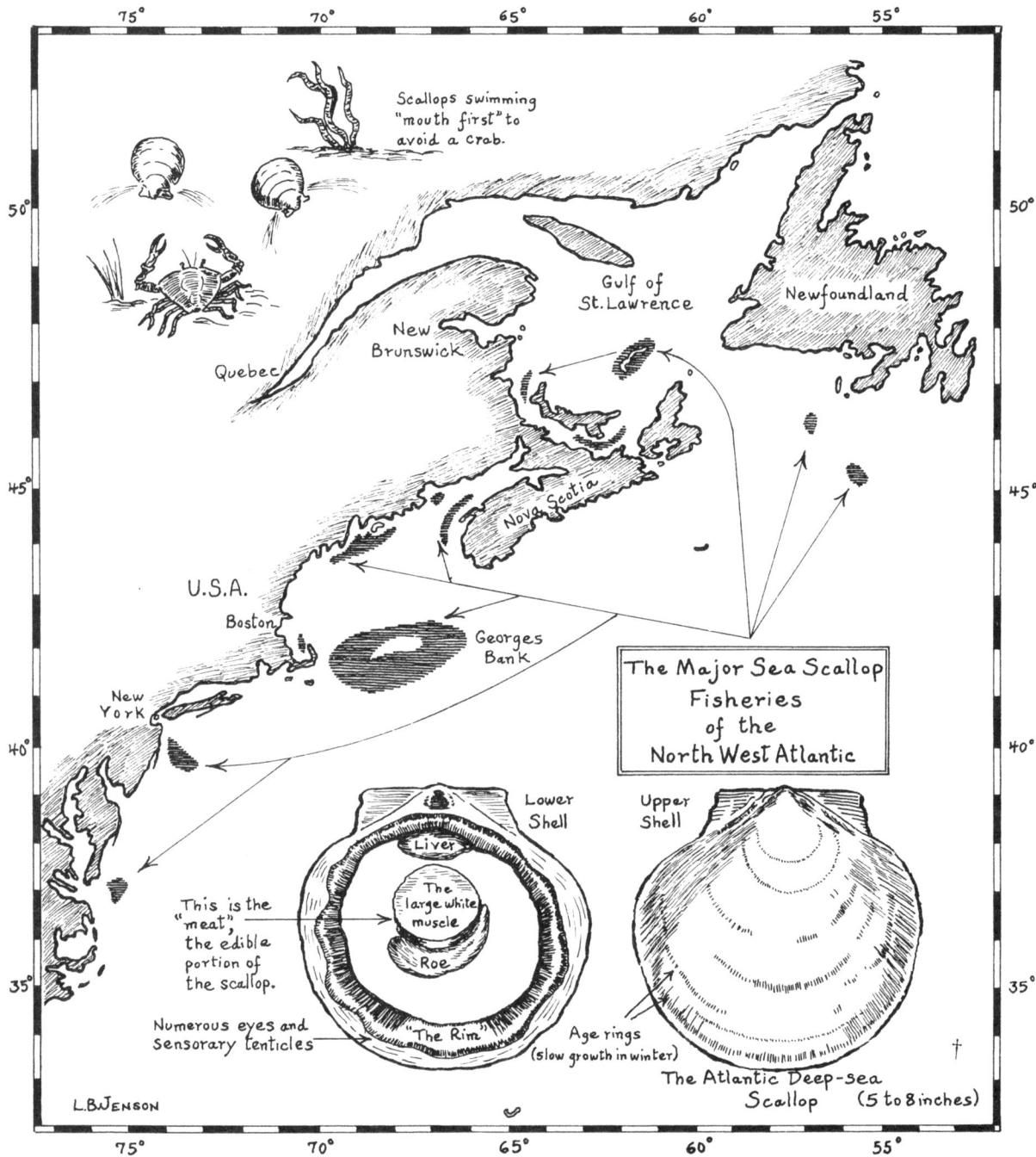

Scallop Dragger "Sharon Dawn" sailing from Lunenburg in fog for the fishing banks *

An Offshore Scallop Dragger

The scallop rakes are dragged from the blocks on the gallows, one port & one stb'd. The two booms are used when the rakes are recovered to lift them up so that the contents may be spilled on the deck.

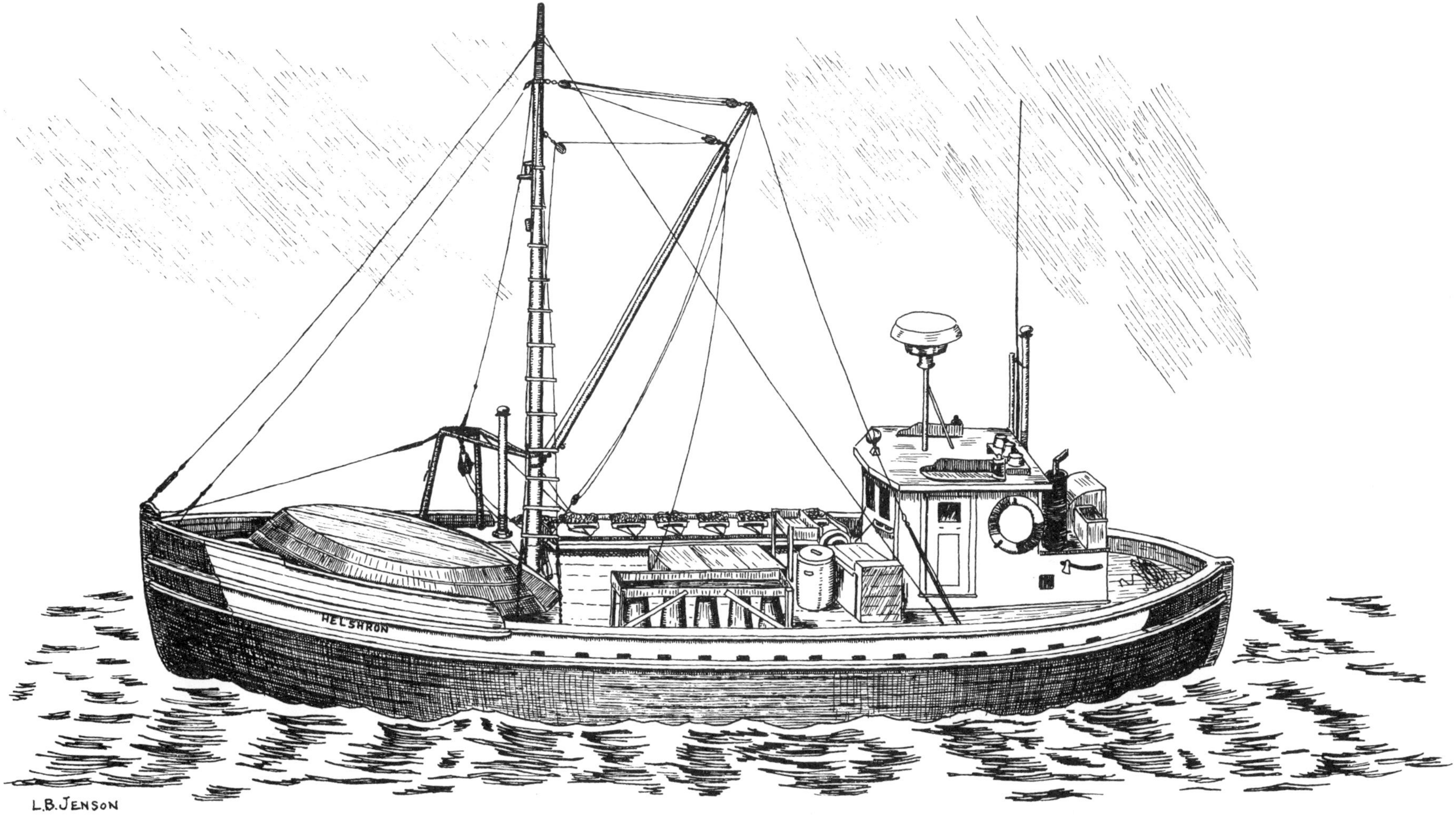

A 50 foot Digby Inshore Scallop Dragger

Scallops are dragged from the sea bottom by 6 or 7 steel mesh bags on a bar towed from a gallows on the starboard side (protected by 3 inch hardwood sheathing). The boom is used for lifting the bags for emptying on to the wooden platform on deck. When the scallops are shucked the wooden platform is tipped up to dump the shells and other debris overboard.

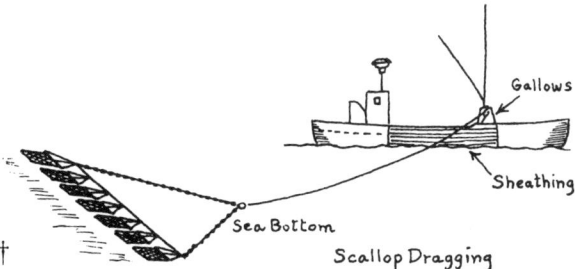

Scallop Dragging

Scallop bags about to be emptied

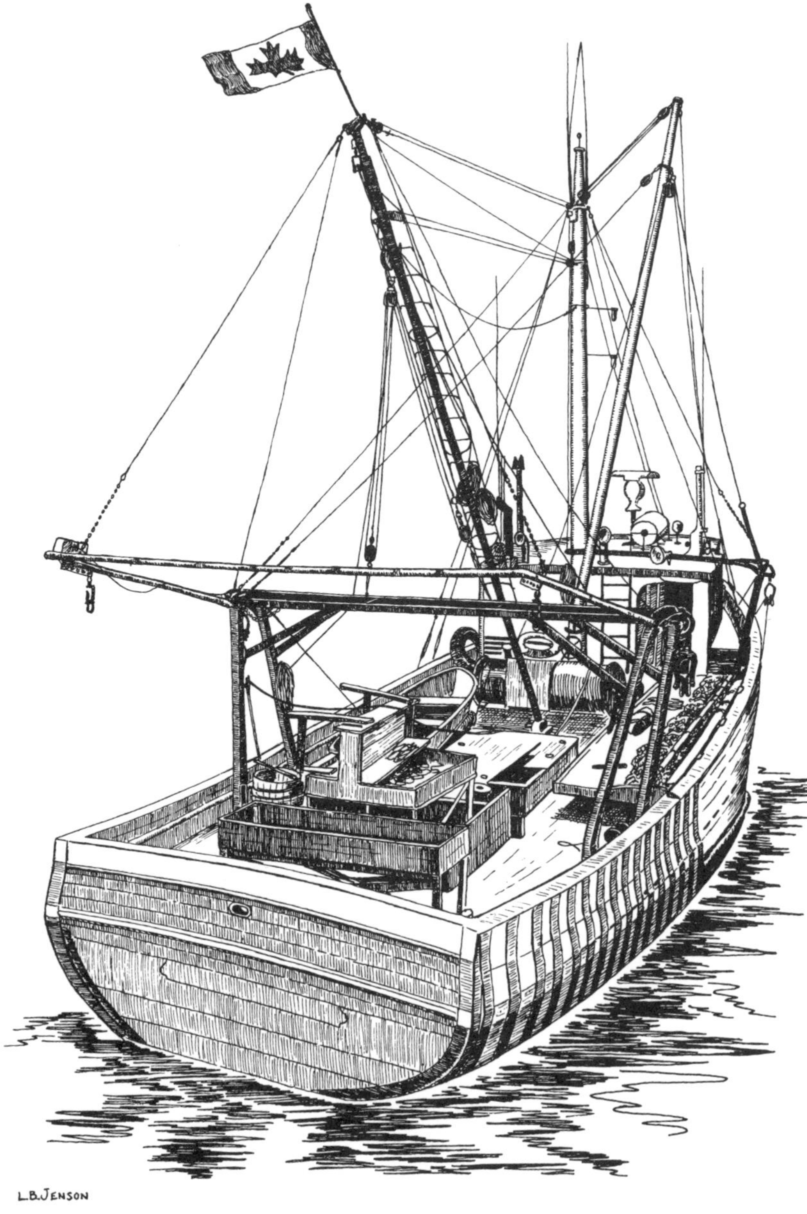

Stern view of a 60 foot Digby Dragger
She is rigged for scallop dragging. The doors
for stern trawling have been landed.

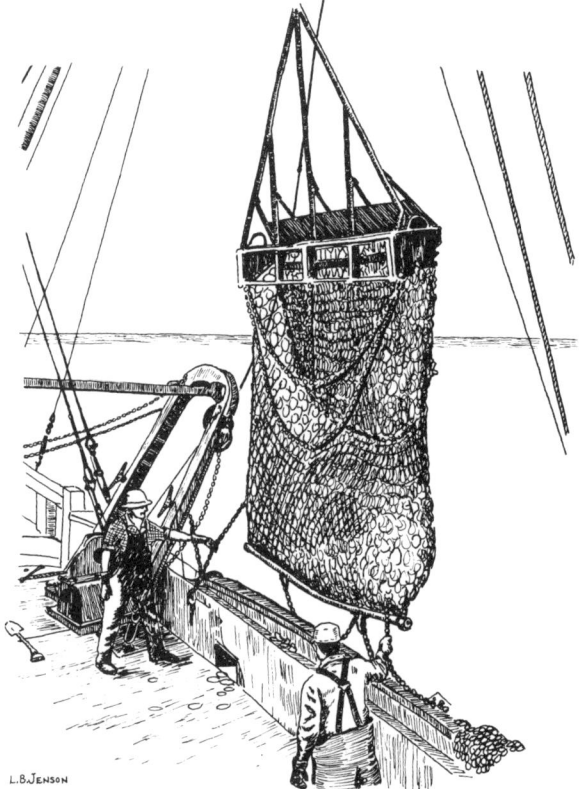

† Bringing an offshore 12 foot Scallop Drag on board.

L.B. JENSON

† The Otter Trawl "doors" & gallows are seen on deck at the stern.

A 60 foot Stern Dragger
Nova Scotia, Bay of Fundy
Used inshore and offshore for stern trawling for groundfish. She also can be fitted for scallop dragging and for longlining.

A Canadian Stern Fishing Trawler

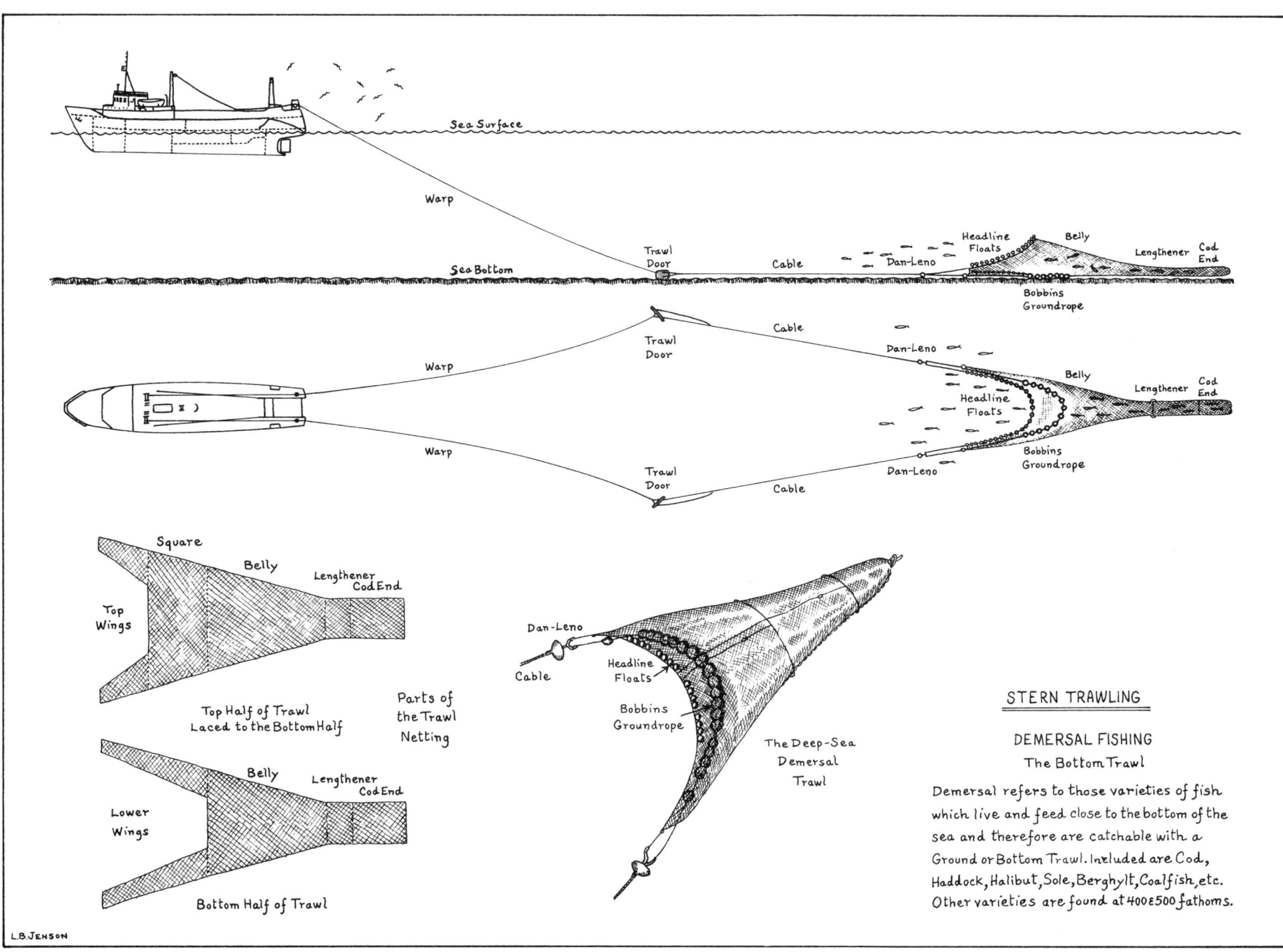

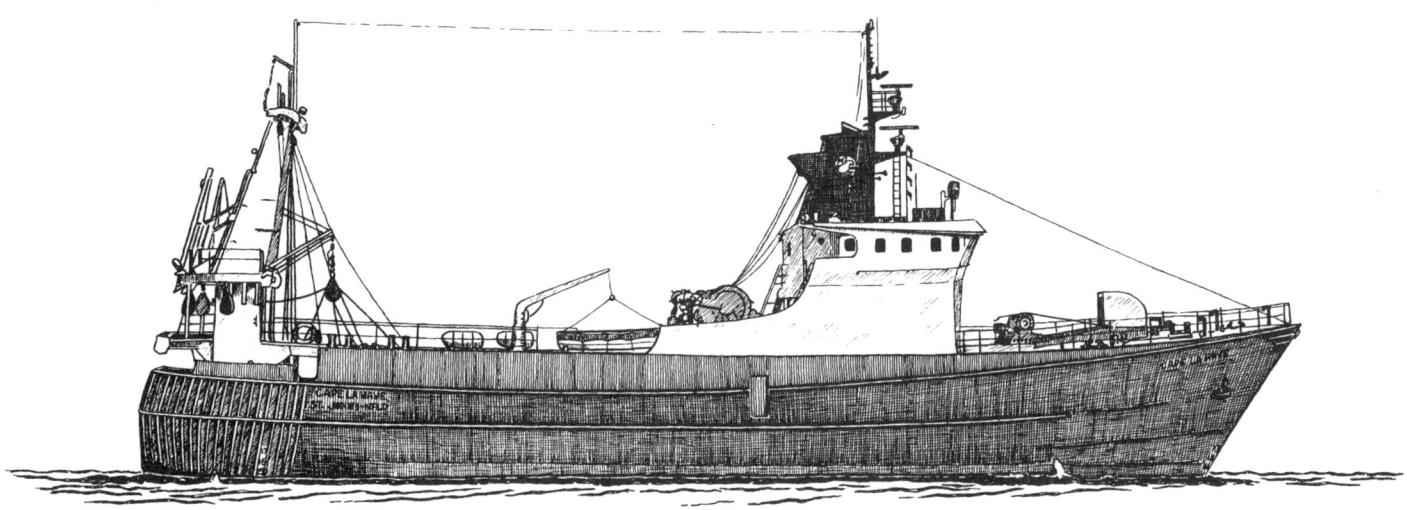

"CAPE LA HAVE"

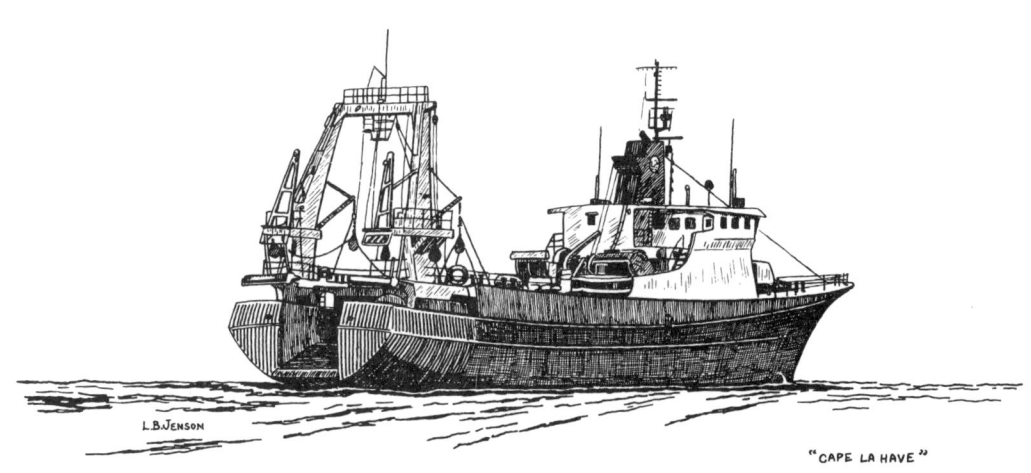

"CAPE LA HAVE"

Stern Trawler "CAPE LA HAVE" †
Built 1973, Capacity 400,000 pounds of fish.

The Bridge of Cape Argos, first North American Midwater Trawler. The experience, knowledge, perseverience and intuition of the Captain aided by electronic fish finders and other instruments ranged on the Bridge are the key to success for these vessels.
It is said that it also helps if the Captain thinks like a fish!

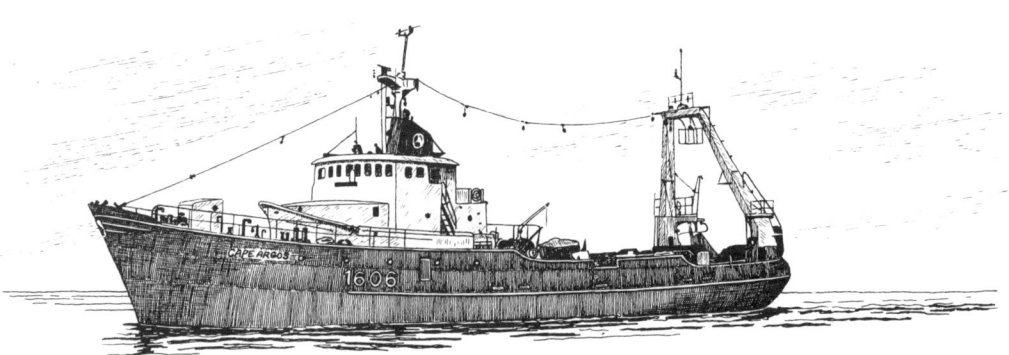

"CAPE ARGOS"

Hauling in the Cod End of a Mid Water Trawl
30,000 pounds of fish after a 2 hour trawl

L.B. Jenson (from a NSCIC photo)

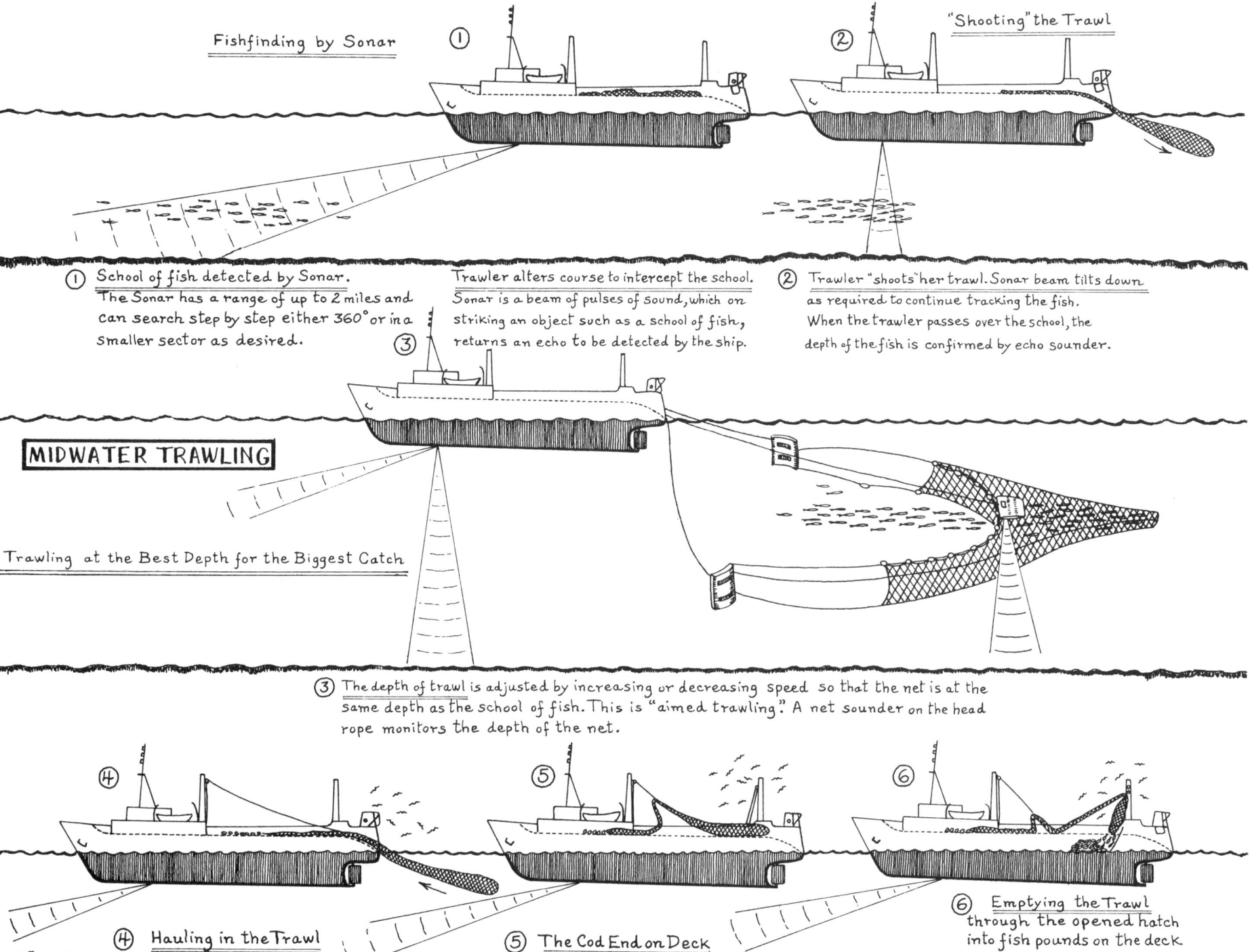

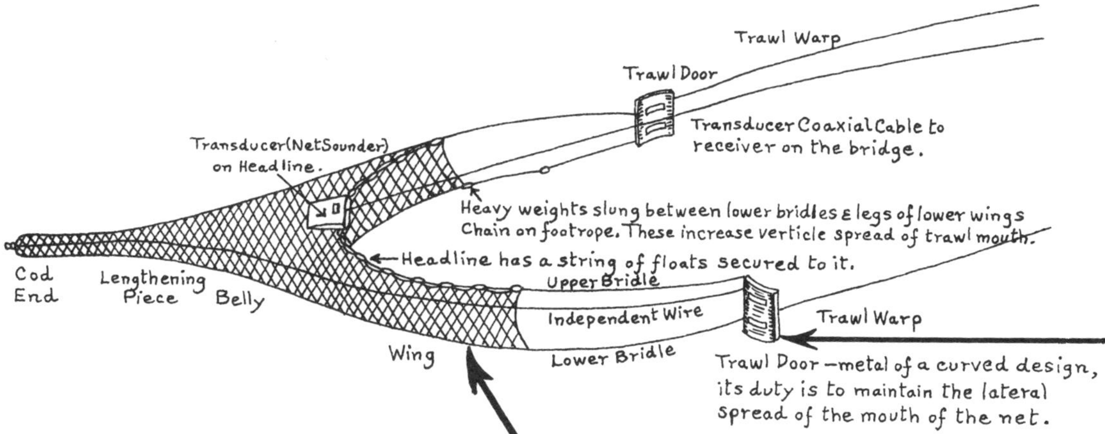

The Pelagic Trawl

Pelagic refers to those varieties of fish which live in midwater and are not catchable with ground trawls. Included are Herring, Mackerel, Sprats, Sandeels etc. The Pelagic Trawl is much larger than a Bottom Trawl. It is made up of a top half and a bottom half and two side panels i.e. four large tapering pieces with long wings. A standard design is not fixed as yet.

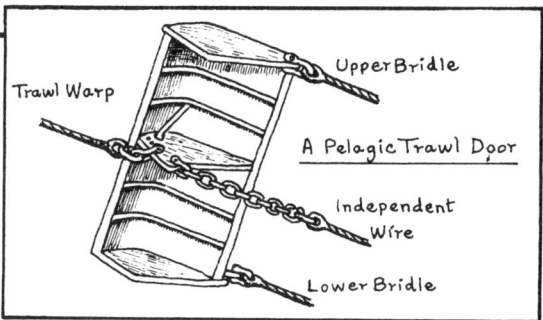

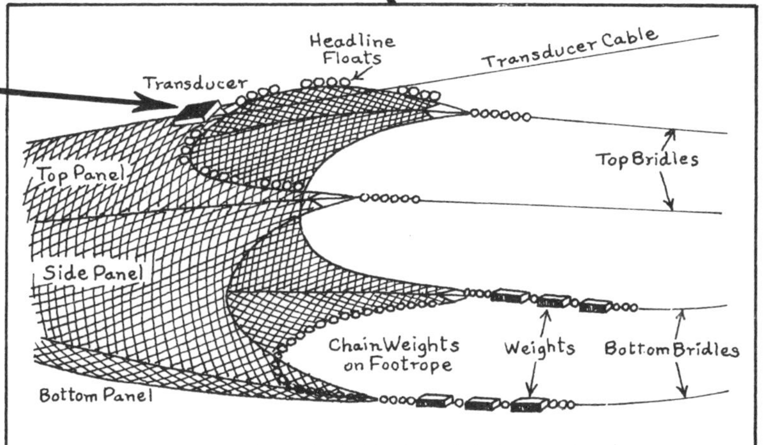

A Pelagic Trawl Door

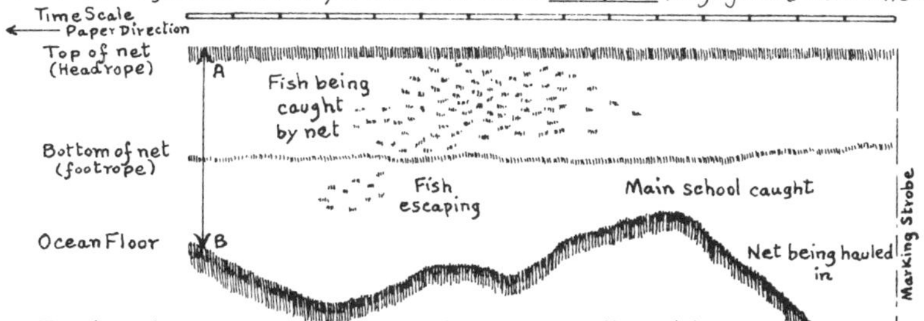

PELAGIC FISHING
The Midwater Trawl
Fishfinding, Tracking and Netting using Sonar, Echo Sounding and Net Sounding

Midwater trawls are much lighter than bottom trawls, are easier to shoot and tow and are less susceptable to damage. Nets are longer and have a high, wide opening for larger catches. In addition to midocean depths, midwater trawls can work near rough bottoms which are quite inaccessable to bottom trawls. In addition to their main function, net sounders indicate how full the net is, if the net is fouled, burst or the cod end opened.

L.B. JENSON

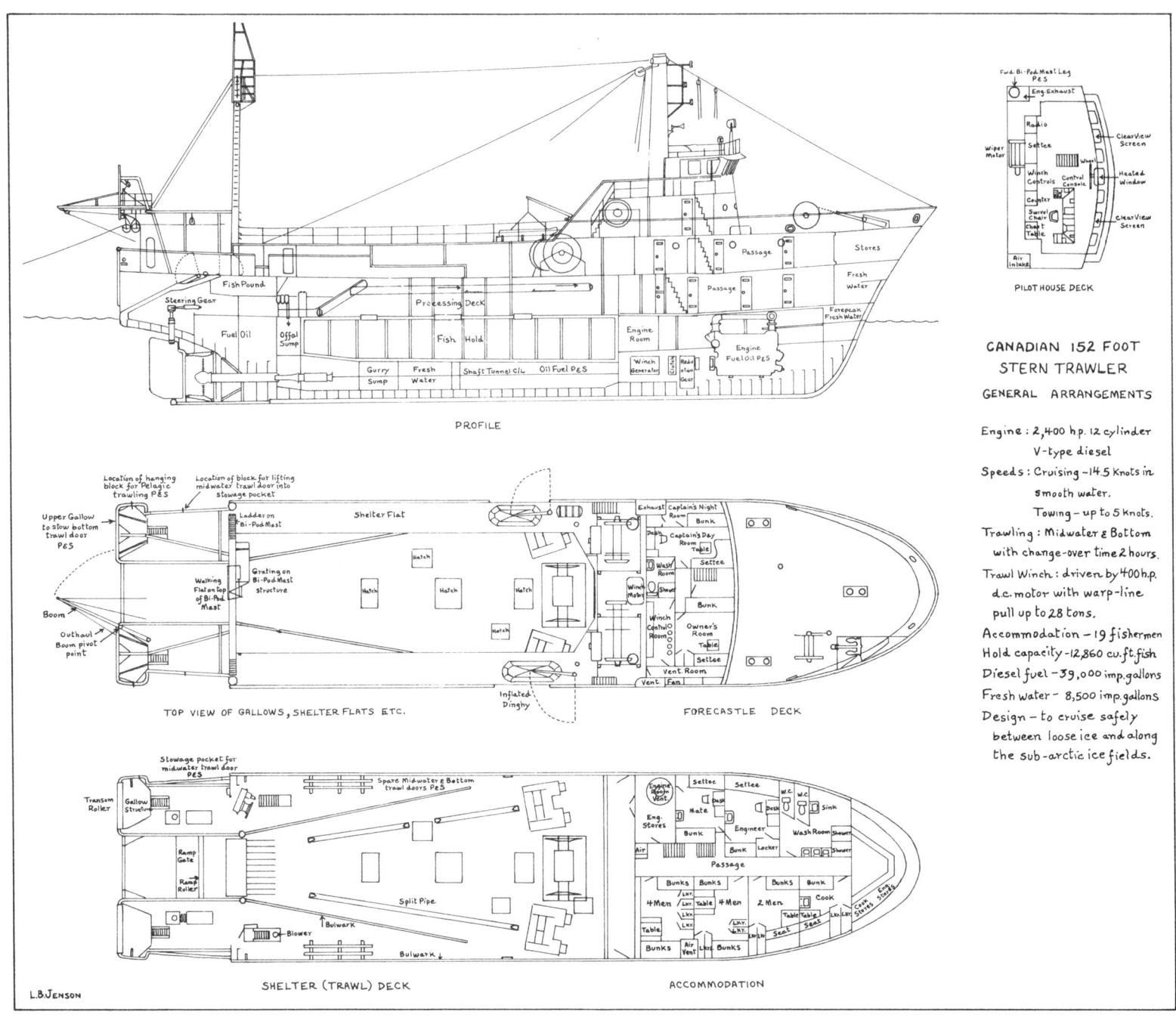

IRISH MOSS
(CHONDRUS CRISPUS)

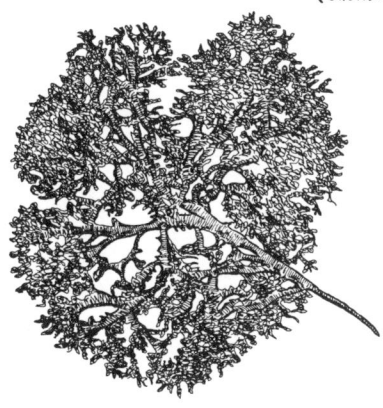

Plant colours range from dark red-purple to greenish to beige; length is 2 to 4 inches (5-10cm). Irish Moss is found near the low tide mark in pools and on rocks of Atlantic coastal waters. The peak harvest is in spring and summer. To forage Irish Moss simply rake by hand at low tide from a boat or collect the storm-tossed weeds from the beaches. Dry the Irish Moss in the sun until it is crisp. This ocean vegetable is high in Vitamins A and B1, iodine, most minerals and trace elements.

 Detail of frond

KELP
(ALARIA ESCULENTA)

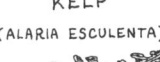

These plants are a dark olive brown in colour. The blades have a midrib & usually are frayed. The stalk is solid with bladelets below the main blade. It grows up to 10 feet long (3m). Kelp is found on rocks near, or just below the low tide mark. Fresh, storm-tossed plants can be gathered from the beaches. Attached plants can be cut from the rocks at low tide. The peak harvest is in spring. Kelp may be used fresh or sun-dried when it should first be hydrated in fresh water. The nutrients are Vitamins B_6 B_{12} and C, sugar, starch, iodine and trace minerals.

DULSE
(PALMARIA PALMATA)

Plants are rose-red to reddish-purple, ranging from about 8 inches to 16 inches tall (20 to 40 cm). Dulse is found growing on rocks, shells etc. from mid tide to low tide mark. The peak harvest is from late spring to mid fall. This ocean vegetable is cut from the rocks at low tide.
Immediately after harvesting dulse should be washed in sea water and then partially dried in the sun and breeze. Dulse is very high in protein, fat and Vitamin A. It contains most minerals and trace elements. Sun-dried dulse often is chewed as a snack.

ROCKWEED or BLADDERWRACK
(FUCUS VESICULOSIS)

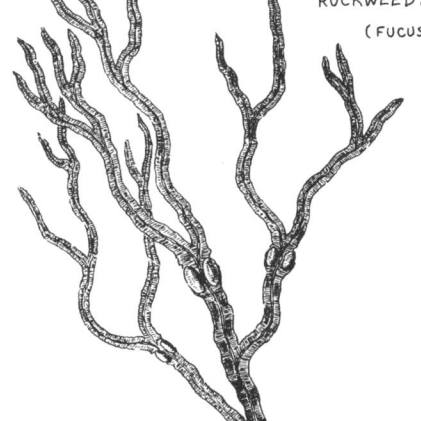

Plants are olive-green and are up to 3 feet (1m) in length. Regularly branched with air bladders, they have a leathery texture. Rockweed prefers an exposed location on rocks near the low tide mark. It should be harvested in early fall for a very high Vitamin C content. For a high Vitamin A content it should be harvested in summer. After harvest the fresh plants should be washed, chopped, sun-dried and stored in tight containers. Rockweed contains Vitamins A, C, E and K, most minerals and trace elements. This abundant plant is very widely used along the coast as a garden fertilizer.

L.B. JENSON

Irish Moss is a particularly valuable plant. It has a high content of gelose or carrageenin, a jelly-like substance with an infinite number of uses, including preparation of soups, jellies, creams, paint, ink & ointments.

SOME SEAWEEDS OF NOVA SCOTIA

The architecture of the old seaport of Lunenburg

Schooners at anchor and alongside in Lunenburg — 1920's

L.B. Jenson

Lunenburg County Academy — built in 1895.

Dory Racing in Lunenburg

The Overhanging Dormers
— of Lunenburg —
This feature of architecture
is unique to Lunenburg County

L.B. Jenson

Mr. Everett Lohnes, Pelham Street, Lunenburg.
Sailmaker for over 60 years for Banks schooners.

Thomas Walters & Son, Kempt St. & Montague, Lunenburg.
Blacksmiths for 100 years
Manufacturers of ironwork for schooners.

THE OLD FISHING PORT OF LUNENBURG
FOUNDED 1753

The Romkey House — built before 1783.
It is the oldest house still standing in
Lunenburg. In the 1800's it was the Customs
Office for the Port.

Alfred Dauphinee & Sons, Lunenburg.
Blocks, Oars and Marine Hardware.
Manufacturers of lignum vitae deadeyes etc. for schooners.

SEALING

- Canadian seal quota regulations permit <u>two vessels</u> from Nova Scotia to take part in the annual seal hunt. <u>Four vessels</u> from Newfoundland also hunt seals, together with <u>three</u> from Norway. Landsmen also hunt harp seals.
- <u>The main seal hunt</u> takes place on the icefields off southern Labrador.
- <u>Harp Seals</u> — most of the harps taken are pups, known as "whitecoats." The Canadian quota is 56,000. Norway's quota of harps is 20,000.
- <u>Hood Seals</u> — these congregate further offshore than the harps. Their pups are known as "bluebacks." The combined quota for Canada & Norway is 15,000.
- "Martin Karlsen" returned to Blandford, Nova Scotia, from the 1979 hunt about 7th April, 1979, with 10,000 pounds of seal pelts. The pelts were landed at the Karlsen Fish Plant where the fat was separated from the skins. The fat was rendered to be used in making margarine and in non-dairy whipping cream. The residue of protein could be an additive for products such as cornflakes or animal feed.
- <u>The skins</u> were sold overseas to Japan, England and Norway to be used in the manufacture of belts, purses & other leather goods.
- <u>The Karlsen Fish Plant</u> employs about 50 workers. In season, the plant deals in salt herring and frozen mackerel for direct sale to markets overseas. The crew of "Martin Karlsen" were Newfoundlanders.
- <u>The seal meat & flippers</u> were sold in Newfoundland to Canada Packers. Seal flippers are considered a seasonal delicacy in Newfoundland.
- <u>The Annual Seal Hunt</u> is the world's last remaining Great Hunt. Past such hunts come to mind — awks, passenger pigeons, buffalo, caribou, whales etc. It is hoped that the Canadian Government biologists who determine seal hunt quotas have all their facts correct.
- It is certainly true that the Annual Seal Hunt provides seasonal employment for a substantial number of Canadians and is of value to the Canadian economy. With good management the future of the seals should be assured and the hunt should continue with benefits of employment and trade.

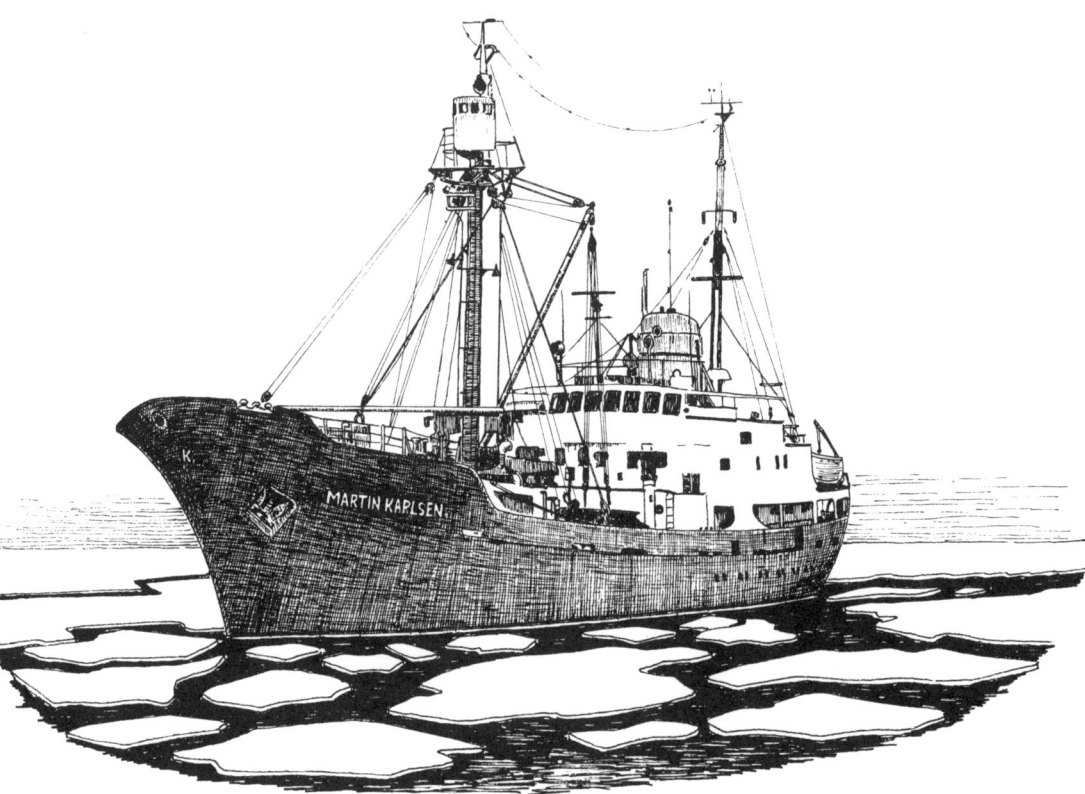

THE SEAL HUNT 1979
"MARTIN KARLSEN" out of BLANDFORD, NOVA SCOTIA

L. B. JENSON

The ancient Norse peoples believed that seals had the mysterious powers to turn into maidens at night & fancied that they could hear them singing on the ledges and island shores.

When I was a young man in charge of a Naval picket boat, I often had to remain in my 50 foot boat during heavy gales in Scapa Flow in the Orkney Islands (in case my boat broke adrift). Almost always a Harbour Seal would come alongside and keep me company for hours on end.

I was pleased to see a Harbour Seal in St. Margaret's Bay just as I was preparing this drawing. I suspect my fishermen friends would not be so pleased.

The Harbour Seal (or Common Seal) is about 6 feet long and may weigh up to 250 pounds. They appear dark when wet but when they are dry their colour varies from gray to brown and red. There perhaps are 5,000 around Nova Scotia. In the State of Maine there used to be a bounty of $1.00 per Harbour Seal. By 1910 they were nearly exterminated. There was no noticable effect on fish catches. Harbour Seals now, can only be taken by permit. They live in bays and near inshore ledges.

Gray Seals (or Horsehead Seals) are about 8 feet long and weigh up to 800 pounds. They are gray or brown in colour but all appear gray when they are wet. The most distinctive feature is the "Roman" or "horsehead" nose. In captivity they have lived for more than 40 years. Normally they inhabit exposed offshore rocky ledges.

The beautiful Harp Seal is about 6 feet long and weighs about 400 pounds. They are light cream or white in colour with dark patches in a harp-shaped pattern. The white-coat pups are clubbed and skinned on the ice by Canadian & Norwegian Sealers. It has to be stated that this is an extremely emotional subject.

Up to 35 million Harps lived in the North Atlantic and Arctic Oceans about 200 years ago. Perhaps 3½ million now can be found. Harp seals normally live in the open seas of the North.

SEALS IN NOVA SCOTIAN WATERS

L.B. JENSON
after Quinn & Tyler

East Ironbound Island Light
This small island is off New Harbour Point between St. Margaret's & Mahone Bays. The first lighthouse here was destroyed by lightning in 1876. The first "light" was 12 candle lamps. These were replaced by two kerosene 2-wick burners. The next was one duplex lamp & lens. In 1965 one chemical-battery electric light & duplex lens were installed. The present mercury vapor light was fitted in 1971. The original hand-operated fog horn was replaced in 1967 by an automatic fog horn. The light stands 146 feet above sea-level & is visable 16 miles. As there is no sheltered harbour, boats have to be hauled up on a skidway. In the old days oxen used to be pushed overboard 25 feet offshore & then they would swim to the Island. The climate is milder than on the mainland & flowers are enjoyed to December. Once 9 families lived there.

SAMBRO ISLAND LIGHTHOUSE
(off entrance to Halifax Harbour)
and
COAST GUARD LIFECRAFT 117

Sambro Island is an 8 acre, solid granite rock 3½ miles off the coast. It is surrounded by a great number of rocks & shoals which have destroyed many ships & claimed hundreds of lives. The first lighthouse here was built in 1759. The present light is 82 feet high & is visable for 17 miles. Coast Guard Lifecraft now are stationed at several points in Nova Scotia & already have saved many lives. Markings on these vessels have been altered since 1978

L.B. JENSON

The Magdalen Islands & Sable Island are remote spots, but familiar to many of our fishermen. Sable Island has claimed many ships & lives. Many years ago my own ship took a closer look than I intended...............

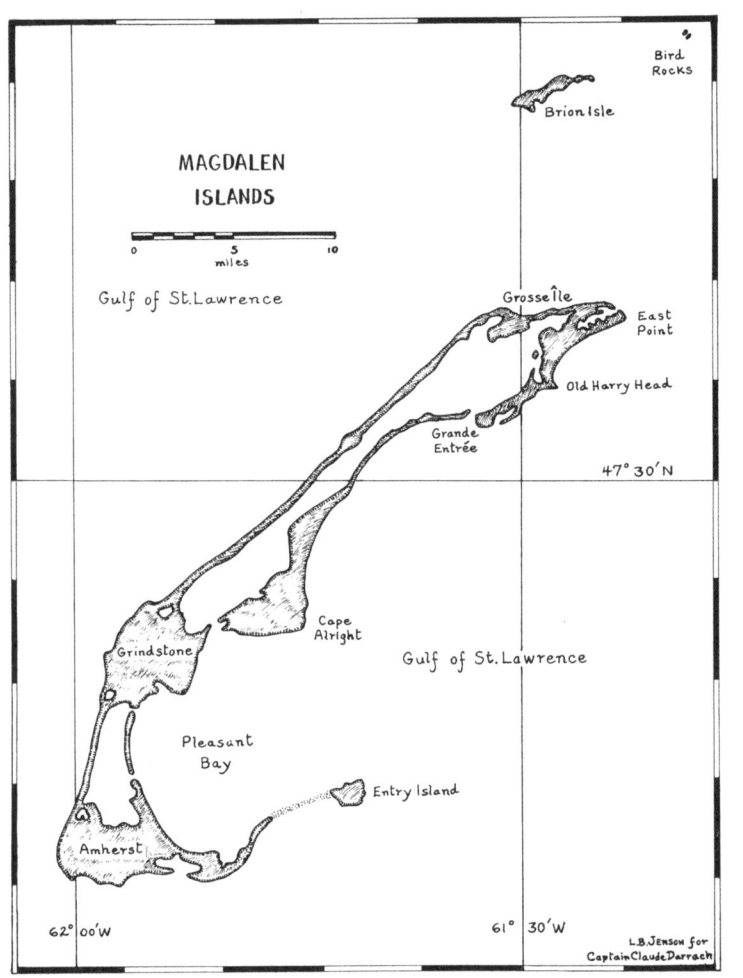

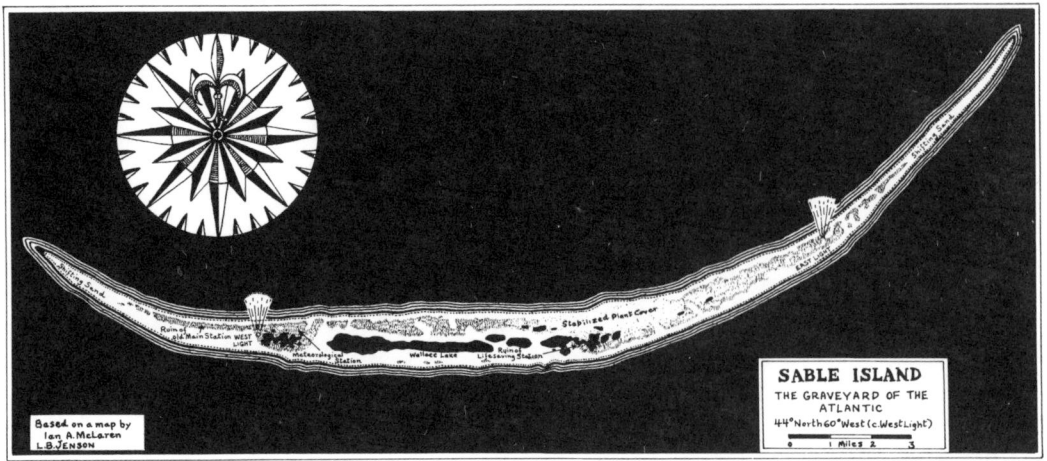

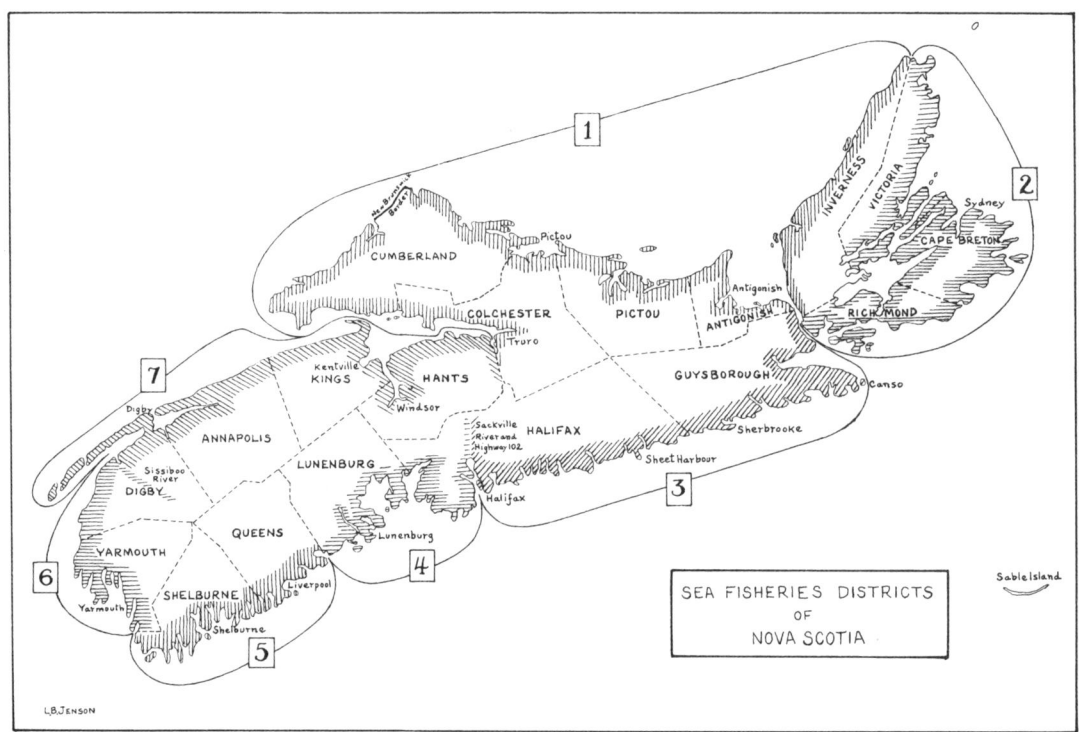

Under the floor of the North West Atlantic there may be vast quantities of oil. Where once there were only fishing vessels we now may find special ships & platforms drilling for oil. The effect, if any, on fishing has yet to be determined. (1980)

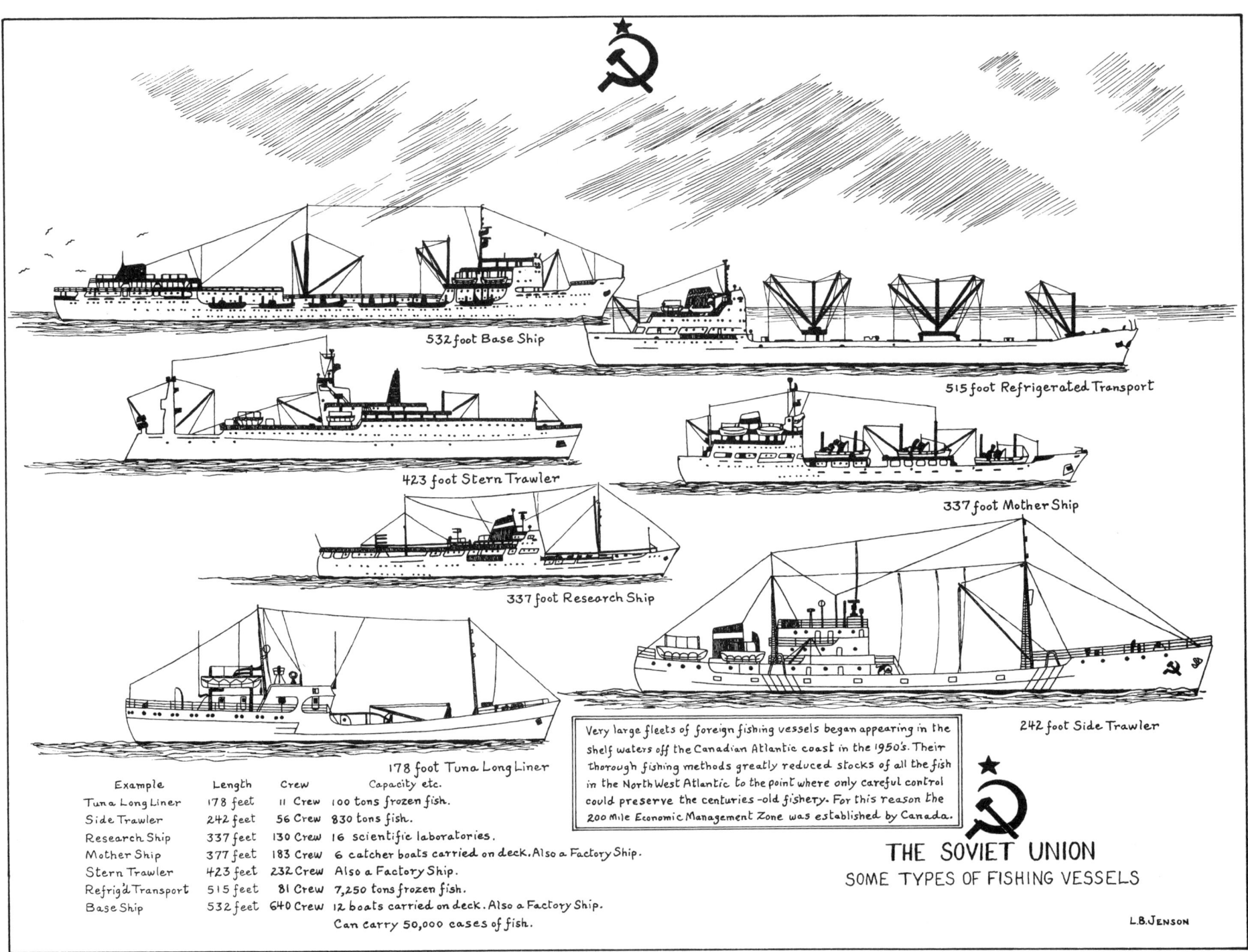

 Jellyfish

```
         The Nova Scotian Fishing Fleet
              (figures for 1977)
  Inshore Fleet    30 to 44 feet in length    2,452 Vessels
  Midshore Fleet   45 to 64 feet in length      150 Vessels
  Offshore Fleet   65 to 139 feet in length     180 Vessels
                                     Total   2,752

  Main Concentrations of Vessels
  Shelburne County      604 vessels (22%) 92% are less than 44 feet
  Region 8 (Yarmouth Cty. to Weymouth) 499 vessels (18%)
  Pictou & Antigonish Counties    385 vessels (14%)
  Digby County       42 vessels 45 to 64 feet — Midshore Vessels
  Lunenburg County   Largest concentration of Offshore Vessels
```

THE NORTHWEST ATLANTIC FISHERIES

.... 100 fathom line

THE 200 MILE FISHERIES ZONE

FISHERIES PROTECTION

It is of vital importance that quotas for fish catches are observed, that vessels do not fish on banned spawning grounds and that all the other regulations of the Federal Department of Fisheries and Oceans are observed. If they are not observed it is not likely that our fish stocks ever will recover from past overfishing.

Three Department of Fisheries Patrol Vessels are based in Halifax. CGS Chebucto and CGS Cygnus are used for surveillance of offshore waters to the limit of the 200 mile economic zone. CGS Louisbourg is used to patrol the inshore fisheries.

In 1979 the patrol ships boarded 477 fishing vessels for inspection and participated in 61 search and rescue incidents.

These ships are a deterrent to those who would break fishing rules. Any foreign ships believed to be ignoring Canadian regulations can be "invited" into a Canadian port. The possibility of loss in fishing time offsets possible economic gains from illegal fishing. Only time and experience will determine how strong our fisheries patrols should be.